GARDENING
MADE EASY

GARDENING
MADE EASY

Katie and Gene Hamilton

Illustrated by Lauren Jarrett

ADAMS MEDIA CORPORATION
Holbrook, Massachusetts

First Adams Media Corporation edition published in 1996.

Published by Adams Media Corporation
260 Center Street, Holbrook, MA 02343

ISBN: 1-55850-583-0
Printed in the United States of America

First Edition
J   I   H   G   F   E   D   C   B   A

Library of Congress Cataloging-in-Publication Data
Hamilton, Katie.
Gardening made easy / Katie and Gene Hamilton : illustrated by Lauren Jarrett.
p.   cm.
Originally published: Garden City, N.Y. : Doubleday Book & Music Club, 1994.
ISBN: 1-55850-583-0 (pbk.)
1. Backyard gardens. 2. Landscaping gardening. 3. Gardening.
I. Hamilton, Gene. II. Title.
[SB473.H298   1996]
635.9—dc20   95-51782
CIP

This publication is designed to provide accurate and authoritative information with regard to the subject matter covered. It is sold with the understanding that the publisher is not engaged in rendering legal, accounting, or other professional advice. If legal advice or other expert assistance is required, the services of a competent professional person should be sought.
— From a *Declaration of Principles* jointly adopted by a Committee of the American Bar Association and a Committee of Publishers and Associations

Cover photo credit: Lefever/Grushow from Grant Heilman Photography, Inc.

This book is available at quantity discounts for bulk purchases.
For information, call 1-800-872-5627.

Visit our home page at http://www.adamsmedia.com

Acknowledgments

We wish to thank several organizations for help with this book: Ames Lawn and Garden Tools, Parkersburg, WV; Canadian Sphagnum Peat Moss Assn., St. Albert, Alberta, Canada; National Garden Bureau, Downers Grove, IL; Netherlands Flower Bulb Information Center, Brooklyn, NY; NK Lawn and Garden Co., Minneapolis, MN; and the United States Department of Agriculture, Washington, DC.

We are especially pleased to have the fine art of Lauren Jarrett illustrating this book, and editing by W. L. Broecker and Karen Murgolo. As always we appreciate the support and guidance from our friend and agent, Jane Jordan Browne.

Table of Contents

Table of Contents

Table of Contents

INTRODUCTION

For some people gardening is therapy, a quiet and rewarding retreat from a fast-paced life. Those who love fresh vegetables say gardening gives them a bountiful harvest unmatched by any store-bought produce. And for practical people like us, gardening is also the means to an end, invigorating and enjoyable work that is part of maintaining house and property.

Tending and nurturing flowers and vegetables does not require an acre spread or an expansive backyard. Looking around any city reveals that the balconies of condominiums, apartment windowsills, and rooftops of high-rise buildings display a great variety of containers filled with plants growing with gusto.

To get started in gardening you need to know some basics so the work you put in will produce good-looking, healthy results. That is what *Gardening Made Easy* is all about. It is a handy reference for the first-time home gardener who wants to know how to maintain and care for a yard and garden while saving money by doing it herself or himself.

In this book you'll find 48 basic gardening projects that cover care and maintenance chores, planting basics, and simple things to build for your backyard. Each project explains how to do it fast and do it right with clearly drawn illustrations that show you what's involved. You'll see what tools are most useful for gardening projects and how to use them correctly.

An important connection only you can make is to find a local nursery or garden center where you will purchase plants and materials. You might have to do some shopping around, but it's worth the time it takes to find a plant source you like. If you can plan to do your garden shopping during the week instead of the weekend, you'll find that sales personnel have more time to help you. If you are overwhelmed by what you see walking into a large nursery, don't be bashful and don't be discouraged. Every time you visit you'll become more familiar with the plants, where they are located, and how they are organized.

You might be able to save some money buying gardening materials at grocery or hardware chain stores, since gardening materials are not their

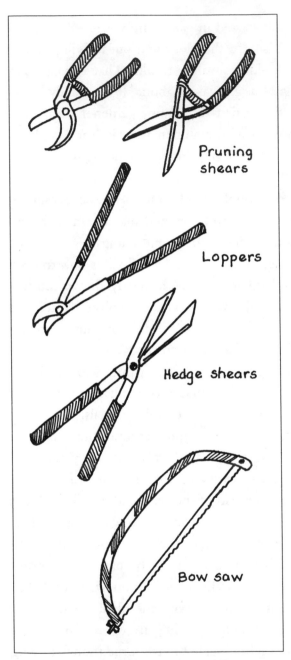

Pruning shears

Loppers

Hedge shears

Bow saw

GARDEN TOOLS AND EQUIPMENT

full-time business you can only hope that the salespeople are knowledgeable. Shopping at a local nursery or garden center pays off for a first-time gardener because that's where you'll get information and answers to your questions from experts with local knowledge.

Once you get in a backyard frame of mind gardening can easily become a passion or a hobby out of control. But let's not get ahead of ourselves. We'll begin with a look at what you need to get started.

GARDENING TOOLS AND EQUIPMENT

Working in a garden requires some basic tools and equipment. You don't have to invest in all of them at one time; purchase them as the need arises. Don't overlook buying used garden equipment. Garage and yard sales are an ideal place to pick up good quality garden tools at bargain prices.

Just how do you know good quality from poor? In general, higher priced tools are better because they're made of heavier, more durable materials. When shopping for garden tools, keep the following points in mind:

• A heavy-gauge steel blade will hold its cutting edge better and will last the longest.

• A wooden handle should be sealed with varnish or other finish to prevent moisture damage and provide a smooth gripping surface.

• A tool head with a socket that fits over the end of the handle is strongest and will resist breaking.

❧ Cutting, Trimming, and Pruning Tools

Pruning shears are small, hand-held snippers used for cutting away excess or dried ends of woody plants and shrubs. They are designed to cut small and medium-sized shoots and branches. Don't try to cut through a branch that barely fits between the blades, and never twist the shears to force them while cutting through a difficult branch. The blades can easily twist beyond straightening-out.

Loppers are heavy-duty pruning shears. They have two arm-length handles that produce high cutting force at the blades. They are used to trim and cut heavy branches pruning shears can't handle.

Hedge shears look like a giant pair of scissors and are suitable for trimming branches of hedges. Because of their long reach and quick straight cuts they are useful garden tools. Choose shears that have a notch in one blade close to the center pivot. This notch helps hold the branch close to the pivot where most cutting leverage is gener-

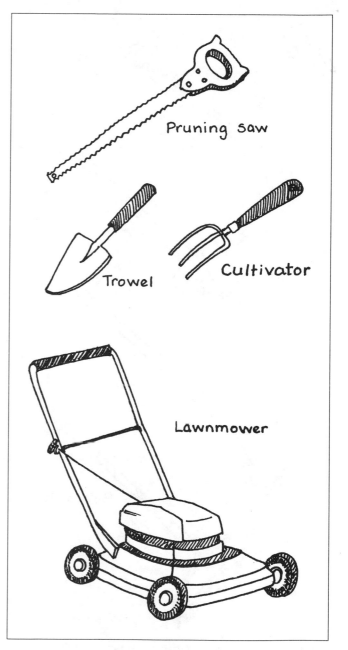

GARDEN TOOLS AND EQUIPMENT

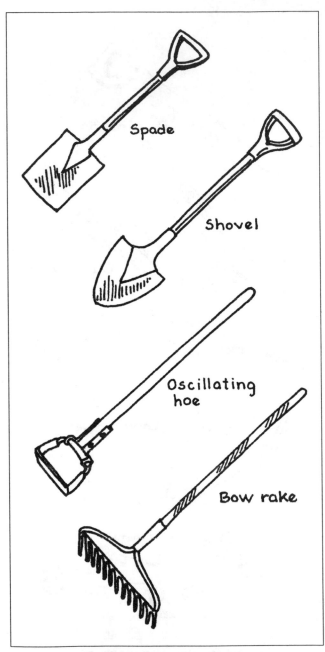

GARDEN TOOLS AND EQUIPMENT

ated and gives better control when trimming large branches.

A bow saw has a steel blade stretched tight across a U-shaped handle that resembles a bow. The thin wide blade has very deep teeth that cut through green wood quickly. Bow saws are used to cut large branches.

A pruning saw has a stiff blade with teeth on both edges and a handle at one end. Fine teeth along one edge are for cutting small branches; large coarse teeth on the other edge are suitable for cutting large branches. Some single-edge pruning saws have a curved handle and a folding blade. Because of their small size they are easy to maneuver in the tight confines of an overgrown bush or shrub.

A lawnmower may be muscle-, gas-, or electrically powered. A musclepowered push mower is ideal for small grass areas or for anyone with a large lawn who wants some exercise while cutting the grass. It is environment-friendly because it uses no gas, oil, or electricity and generates no fumes. Gas and electric mowers range in size from a standard 3.5 hp walk-behind unit to an 18 hp tractor mower that you can ride.

❧ Cultivating, Planting, and Raking Tools

A shovel can be small or large, round or square, scooped or flat. You will need one to dig up soil and move it around. Choose one that is lightweight and has a comfortable handgrip. Don't choose the largest blade you find. With a few more strokes, a small shovel will dig just as large a hole as a large one and is easier and less tiring to handle.

A spade is a shovel with a flat, sharp, straight-edged blade designed for slicing into soil. It is especially good for cutting through tough roots buried beneath the soil and for edging garden beds.

A trowel is a short hand-held scoop used to dig small holes for planting and transplanting. It is also useful for dividing plants and to work the soil in a container.

A long-handled cultivator is a handy tool to break up chunks of hardened soil and to remove weeds. Pull it toward you from back to front.

An oscillating stirrup hoe has a long handle with a stirruplike hinged blade that moves back and forth when you push it through the soil. Its two edges disturb the soil in two directions, making it an efficient cultivator, and will cut through weed roots and other vegetation.

A bow rake has short rigid tines and is used for leveling a bed after digging it up with a shovel or garden fork. Bow rakes will also remove debris and stones from the soil.

A leaf rake, or broom rake, is used for raking leaves, grass clippings, pine needles, and other debris from the lawn and garden bed.

A thatching rake has crescent-shaped blades that you push and pull through a lawn to remove

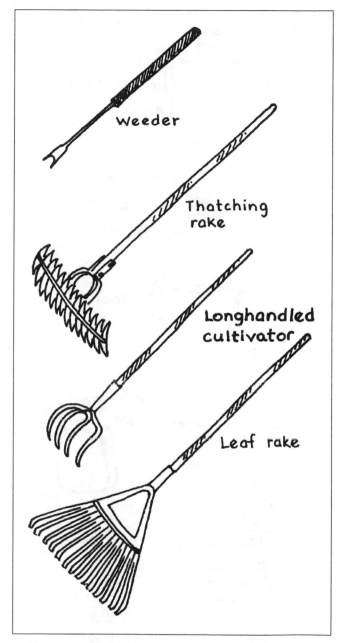

GARDEN TOOLS AND EQUIPMENT

Sprinkling can

Sprinkler

Tool tote

Hose sprayer

Garden hose

GARDEN TOOLS AND EQUIPMENT

dead and matted grass also known as thatch.

A weeder is a hand-held tool used to remove individual weeds in garden beds or the lawn. There are various shapes and designs, but basically a weeder has a wooden or plastic handle attached to a metal shaft about a foot long with a sharp pointed or forked tip. The tip is plunged into the soil to disturb the ground around the weed so it can be removed.

A cultivator is a hand-held tool with three prongs that is used to mix fertilizer into the surface soil or to weed in small, confined areas such as a container or raised garden bed. There are also long-handled cultivators for working the soil while standing.

⁊ Other Equipment

A garden hose with a pistol grip or twist-type nozzle is necessary for watering plants and lawn as well as for washing the car and outdoor furniture. Hoses are $1/2$- or $3/4$-inch–diameter plastic, rubber, or vinyl tubing, sold in lengths of up to 75 feet.

A sprinkler attaches to a hose to dispense water to the lawn and garden beds.

A hose sprayer is a plastic or glass container with a spray nozzle that attaches to the end of a garden hose. It is used to spray fertilizers or pesticides mixed with water.

A utility knife is handy for cutting twine, peat pots, and heavy plastic containers.

A kneeling pad or old pillow is essential to

cushion your knees from the hard, uneven surface of the ground.

A tool tote or a bucket with a handle will keep hand garden tools and gloves in one container that you can move easily wherever you're working.

A wheelbarrow or **utility cart** makes short work of transporting large bags of mulch or several trays of flowers. It is also good for hauling debris to a compost pile.

A sprinkling can is handy for small-area watering and to water plants that need special fertilizer or nutrients.

A drop spreader is a metal or plastic container on a two-wheeled cart with a mechanism for dispensing seed and fertilizer automatically as you walk behind and push it.

A hand-held broadcast spreader is a smaller version of the drop spreader. It is filled with seed or fertilizer; as you walk you turn a handle that dispenses the contents.

❧ Tool Maintenance

Garden tools require very little maintenance to keep them working. They can last a long time if you spend a few minutes keeping them clean, sharp, and lubricated. Here's what to do.

- Remove dirt and mud from tools after each use.
- Remove rust and worn paint from metal parts of tools with a wire brush.
- Use a silicone spray or a water-displacing lu-

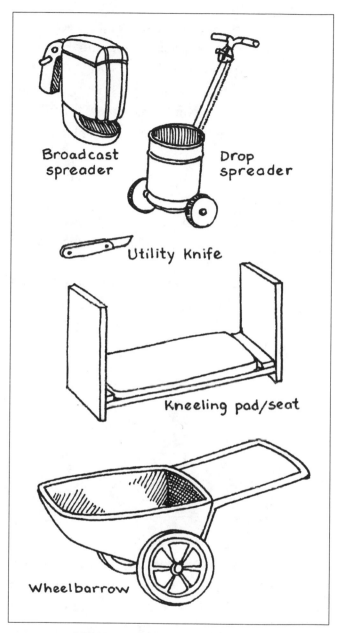

Broadcast spreader

Drop spreader

Utility Knife

Kneeling pad/seat

Wheelbarrow

GARDEN TOOLS AND EQUIPMENT

bricant such as WD-40® to coat exposed metal parts of the tools after each use and especially before extended storage.

• Tighten or replace loose screws, nails, and nuts and bolts as soon as you notice them. If left loose and the tool is used, fasteners can enlarge their mounting holes. In that case, tightening the bolt or screw may not secure the handle, and it may have to be replaced.

• Don't discard a tool because of a broken handle. Most hardware stores and home centers carry replacement handles that are easily installed.

• Shovels and digging tools will work harder with sharp edges. Use a coarse file to hone the cutting edge of the tool. Stroke the file back and forth on both sides of the edge.

GARDENER'S LOGBOOK

A home gardener and the skipper of a boat are both very concerned with weather conditions. Heavy rains and high winds can make a seagoing passage unpleasant; they also can damage your backyard landscape. What the gardener can learn from the captain is how to keep track of conditions, progress, and experiences in a log-book. A gardener's logbook can be a helpful record and a practical planning tool for all kinds of gardening and landscaping projects.

Keeping a logbook can be as simple as jotting down what you planted in a small notebook, or as complex as making daily entries in a detailed diary. As seasons go by your logbook will become the written history of your yard, with all its ups and downs and successes and failures. It's often difficult to remember exactly what you planted, where and when you planted it, and what kind of fertilizer or organic matter was used. Keeping a record, no matter how simple, is useful information to have on hand. A logbook of a garden's progress is also a useful planning tool for future projects because it documents which plants thrived and which didn't in a particular location, such as a shady, damp area.

Choose a notebook that is convenient to use outdoors. A spiral-bound notebook will open flat for easy writing. Pockets in the covers provide handy compartments where you can stow away plant labels and seed envelopes.

A clipboard with looseleaf paper is another option that makes recording garden data easy. The looseleaf sheets can be put into a binder for safe keeping. Another idea is to use a calendar to keep track of your activities. Planning calendars with large blocks available at stationery stores are great for recording information. Designate one calendar for this job and keep track of yard work on it.

You can organize the information in a garden

GARDENER'S LOGBOOK

log by daily or weekly entries like a diary. This will provide a dated accounting of conditions in the yard, what work you accomplished, and possibly a "to do" list of future projects.

Another approach is to set up your log in categories such as vegetables, flower bed, front foun-

dation plantings, and so on. The entries in each category become a mini-diary of specific information about each area of your yard. If you have several major projects going on, this might be the most helpful format to follow, because you can break down the information and refer to it easily.

SECTION I

Easy Care and Maintenance of Your Yard and Garden

WHAT YOU NEED TO KNOW ABOUT SOIL

_K_nowing about the content or composition of your soil is an important first step to understanding why things grow well in your garden, or why they don't.

Soil is a combination of mineral substances or particles formed from the gradual breakdown of rocks, nutrient-rich decaying organic matter, microorganisms, water, and air. All these components are interrelated and make soil a fertile growing environment, with signs of life and activity within it.

All soil is not the same. Good soil is crumbly when you rub it in your hands; it feels granular yet pliable as you work it in the ground. Sand, silt, and clay particles give soil its texture. It needs air for circulation and drainage so water doesn't clog the particles or wash them away.

Soil is generally categorized into three groups: sand, loam, and clay. Ideally your soil will be a mixture of all three but in many instances you will need to amend the soil with organic material or humus to improve its structure.

A clay soil is heavy to the touch when you dig into it, and dense in appearance. When it rains the soil is slow to dry out and because of its denseness it doesn't quickly absorb light and heat from the sun. If you walk through a field or yard with craterlike cracks or ruts, the soil is likely to be clay. It can form a hard crust when left alone, making it almost impenetrable.

A sandy soil is the exact opposite, easy to dig into and composed of visible particles. Rain and sunlight pour through a sandy soil because its light granular texture acts like a sieve.

A loamy soil combines the best features of both clay and sand with humus. Humus is decayed organic matter that improves the structure and the texture of soil. Humus allows soil to retain water and absorb the sun which stimulates plant growth.

❧ Soil Test

Have your soil tested to find out if it is unusually acid or alkaline. The test will tell you the pH level of the soil—the degree of acidity or alkalinity. A neutral pH is 7.0. Soil with a slightly acid pH level of 6.5 is good for both flower and vegetable gardening. The test will also provide a breakdown of how much magnesium, phosphate,

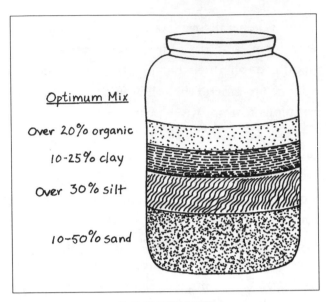

Optimum Mix

Over 20% organic

10-25% clay

Over 30% silt

10-50% sand

HOME SOIL TEST

To get a sample of your soil use a spade or shovel to dig down about 6 inches in a garden and 2 inches in an established lawn. Dig out several examples of soil from throughout the garden or lawn so you'll receive an overview analysis of the entire soil. Pile all the samples of one type together, mix them well, and let them air-dry before packaging them and sending them off.

🍃 Do-it-yourself Soil Test

You can test your soil using a clear quart-size or larger jar with a lid. Fill the jar half full of soil from your garden, then fill the remainder of the jar with water. Tighten the lid and shake it up to mix the soil with the water, then let it sit overnight.

The next day there should be four layers of soil: sand on the bottom, silt next, then clay, and organic matter on the top, either floating in the water or settled onto the clay layer.

Look at the layers in the jar and compare them with the illustration, which shows a good nutrient-rich soil. Add peat moss and/or compost to loosen heavy clay soils or to give body to a sandy soil. Then retest the new soil mixture to see if you've achieved the optimum mix containing at least 20% organic matter.

and potash the soil contains, an analysis of the texture of the soil—sandy, loamy, silty, or clayey —and specific recommendations to enhance it. For example, for a typical flower garden soil with a 6.5 pH, a test may suggest adding 20 pounds of fertilizer per 1,000 square feet.

Local county extension services across the country perform soil testing at very low cost, sometimes as little as $5. Look up your local cooperative extension service under "County Government" in the blue pages of your telephone book. Ask for a soil test kit, which is usually a preprinted mailer and box or sack for the soil sample. Don't combine lawn and garden soil samples together. It's better to submit separate soil tests and label them "lawn," "flower garden," or "vegetable patch" as appropriate.

FERTILIZING PLANTS

Fertilizers are a diet supplement for plants that help them prosper. They are organic or chemical materials that when combined with the soil nurture healthy plant growth. The vital nutrients that they supply are taken up by the root hairs of the plant and are transmitted by the cell system throughout the stem, leaves, and blossoms of the plant.

Chemical fertilizers come in dry or liquid form. You spread dry fertilizers (granules, powders, crystals, and pellets) on the soil and then lightly water most types to mix them into the soil. Some slow-release dry fertilizers are not activated by water, but are left dry to add nutrients over a longer period of time. Fertilizer stakes and tablets also are available. These are driven into the soil surrounding a shrub or tree and release their nutrients into the soil slowly as they dissolve.

Liquid fertilizers are mixed with water and applied with a watering can or sprayed from a hose sprayer. Some are applied to the leaves of the plant so nutrients are taken up quickly.

Drop spreaders

Hand-held broadcast spreaders

SPREADERS

❧ N-P-K

A group of three numbers found on packages of fertilizers indicate the percent ratio of the most important nutrients for plants: nitrogen (N), phosphorous (P), and potassium (K). For example, 5-10-5 means the fertilizer is 5 percent nitrogen, 10 percent phosphate, and 5 percent potassium; the rest of the mix is filler material. N-P-K ratios differ; the proper ratio for your garden will depend on the soil composition and the kind of plants you are growing. Ask for advice at your garden or lawn center. A fertilizer with a combination of the three is considered a complete fertilizer.

❧ Organic Fertilizers

Organic fertilizers such as peat moss, bone meal, manure, and composted materials release nutrients naturally as they decompose in the soil and consequently do not harm our rivers and waterways. They are easy to use and readily available. They are usually more expensive than chemical fertilizers but they add more organic matter to the soil without needing continued watering, which can be costly.

Two useful organic materials to add to your yard and garden are sphagnum peat moss and humus. Sphagnum peat moss helps the soil store fertilizers and release them slowly, and it improves the soil's ability to retain water. Moisten it thoroughly with water, then mix it into the soil. Humus, the end result of composting, is decomposed plant and animal matter that binds soil particles together and helps to aerate the soil. It too is mixed into the soil around a plant.

❧ When Should You Fertilize?

In general, feed nutrients to planted material when it is actively growing. Treat plants and trees with chemical fertilizers in the spring when putting in new garden beds or landscaping materials. Since organic matter decomposes slowly, adding it to soil in the fall is a good idea. The material has all winter to decay and enrich the soil before a spring planting.

Using an organic fertilizer named Hollytone® as an example, the label gives specific measurements of pounds or cups of fertilizer for various applications. For example, it suggests that to feed a shrub, use one cup per foot of branch spread. For a tree it suggests one pound of Hollytone per inch of trunk diameter.

For fertilizers that require being mixed with water, it's handy to have a gallon bucket and a measuring cup. For covering large areas consider using your garden hose with a hose-end sprayer attachment. For small areas or one particular plant or grouping, the sprinkling can works effectively.

Fertilizer tablets and stakes are another option and produce a long lasting source of nutrients to plants and trees by working underground providing nutrients to their feeder roots. It's important to space stakes or "spikes" of fertilizer equally around a shrub or tree so the nutrients are evenly distributed. Package instructions on Jobe's® Fertilizer Spikes for Evergreens, for example, suggest the number of spikes needed for the diameter of the tree.

❧ Application

Whatever type of fertilizer you choose, read and follow the directions on the label. Application instructions are usually clearly written with exact amounts suggested for use in various situations. Instructions tell you how and when to apply them for the best results.

Some instructions say to add the fertilizer in a single application, others suggest smaller doses throughout the season. These instructions are there to give you the best results, so heed their words.

The most precise method of applying dry fertilizers is with a push-type garden spreader, also called a drop spreader. This kind of spreader is ideal for applying fertilizer to large areas. A hand-held broadcast spreader can also be used. This is a plastic container with a crank on its side that spins a dispensing wheel to throw the fertilizer around in a circular pattern. Hand-held spreaders are less expensive than the drop type and can be stored on a shelf. Since spreaders are used only a couple of times a year, finding a place to park a drop spreader when it's not being used can be a problem if you don't have a storage shed or garage.

Use caution Always use caution when applying chemical fertilizers. Heed all warnings on the label, read the entire package, front, sides, and back. If the "Caution" section of the label says to wash your hands after use, be sure to do so. Always keep fertilizers out of the reach of children, and secure against spilling onto other surfaces.

MULCH

Spreading mulching material throughout your garden is one of the best long term invest-

MULCHING

ments you can make in the soil. Mulch is a covering layer that conserves moisture, suppresses weeds, reduces water runoff, and prevents erosion. While doing these tasks, mulch creates a rich, unified background for plants, shrubs and trees. When it decomposes, mulch becomes a valuable addition to the soil structure. Mulch never stops working for you or paying off.

Sun and wind work together to dry out garden beds and vegetable patches. A layer of mulch acts as an insulator to keep the soil cool, which reduces evaporation and conserves moisture. So the damaging drying effects of sun and wind are checked. When it rains, instead of washing the soil away the rain seeps into the mulch and from there into the soil.

In winter months the soil in a garden heaves from the effects of repeated freezing, thawing, and refreezing; this cycle can also damage plants and shrubs. An insulating layer of mulch helps reduce soil damage and the danger to plants from the freeze-thaw cycle.

Mulch works slowly over a period of time, so many of its benefits are not readily visible. However you will notice how mulch cuts down on the growth of weeds by choking them out. And those weeds that sprout up through the mulch seem easier to deal with, perhaps because they're clearly visible. To pull them, spread the mulch away from the weed so you have clear access. As you pull out the weed make sure to get all of its roots so none are left in the ground or that its seeds don't drop into the mulching material. When the area is clear, respread the mulch in a smooth layer.

🌿 Mulching Materials

Organic mulch improves the structure of the soil as it eventually breaks down and begins to decompose. The decomposing mulch releases valuable plant nutrients into the soil. As mulching material deteriorates it turns into a dark color and becomes a rich humus that enriches the soil.

In choosing a mulch consider first what is available in your region and what it costs. The best place to look at different types of mulches is at a garden center that has open bins displaying the materials. In general, a mulch with coarse particles remains loose and lasts longer so it's a better choice. Mulches with fine particles can become compacted and matted; they also decompose faster, so they do not last as long.

If you're fortunate to have or have access to pine trees, the needles are an excellent mulch. Rake them up and then spread a 3-inch layer throughout your plantings. They're especially attractive surrounding the bases of trees and bushes. Pine needles are acidic, so they make an ideal mulch around shrubs that need an acid soil, such as azaleas and rhododendrons.

Grass clippings can be recycled as mulch when they're dry and shredded. A 2- to 3-inch layer of clippings works nicely; anything thicker can clump and possibly be too much of a covering. Vegetables will benefit from a grass mulch because the clippings are rich in nitrogen. Cut the lawn and let the clippings dry out on the lawn for a day or two. Then shred the clippings by running a lawnmower with a bag over them to cut them up and collect them. Do not use grass clippings that were treated with broad-leaf weed killers. You can mulch your lawn as you mow it using a mulching lawnmower or retrofitting your mower with a mulching blade.

Leaves are an almost inexhaustible source of organic mulch, but they must be ground up. Use a lawnmower with a bag, just as with grass clippings. Spread a 3-inch covering of this fine mulch over the ground.

At your local nursery or garden center you can buy wood bark chips and nuggets in 3-cubic-foot bags. One bag will cover 10 to 12 square feet when spread 2 to 3 inches thick. This can get expensive for a larger area. A better bet is to buy bark chips in bulk. They are sold by the cubic yard with a minimum order. You can save the delivery charge if you have a vehicle suitable for hauling. For on-site delivery the price will vary depending on the quantity you're buying and how far you are from the nursery.

In some communities a local tree nursery, park district, or utility company offers bark chips at a sizable discount. Always check that you're not getting chips from a diseased tree. Some of the most popular other natural materials include straw, hay, and compost.

Generally spread mulching material about 3 inches deep around plants, but don't pack the mulch against plant stems or tree trunks.

Inorganic Mulches

Inorganic mulches include stones, black plastic, and landscape fabric. Stones and marble chips do the same job as organic mulches with one exception. Since they don't decompose they don't have to be replaced. They lend a somewhat more formal look to a landscape and go a long way to warding off weeds. They're often used with plastic sheeting laid beneath them to stifle weed growth.

The pros and cons of black plastic sheeting are always an issue among gardeners. Supporters say the plastic blocks out weed growth and helps to control the temperature of the soil. Many who dislike sheeting say it looks artificial in an otherwise natural setting and that it tears easily and disintegrates. A compromising faction puts down sheeting as a first layer and then conceals it with another kind of mulch. Plastic sheeting is sold in rolls of various widths and lengths, with or without perforated holes so water can reach plant roots and slits or other openings for plants.

Landscape fabrics (see pages 20–22) are an appealing alternative to plastic sheeting because they offer a barrier while allowing water to pass through into the soil. Unlike plastic sheeting, they permit the soil to breathe and absorb oxygen. They are sold in rolls 3 feet and wider, in lengths from 25 to 250 feet. Choose landscape fabric with an ultraviolet (UV) rating, which should make it last longer.

There are various special-use landscape fabrics for vegetables and annuals. Fabrics designed for one-season use are relatively inexpensive. Seed blankets improve germination because they retain moisture and warmth in the soil. Newly planted trees can be protected with 36-inch circles of landscape fabric designed to encircle their bases.

LANDSCAPE FABRIC WITH OPENING FOR PLANT

A BED OF MULCH LAID ON TOP OF THE FABRIC

WORKING WITH LANDSCAPE FABRIC

Landscape fabric is tough stuff, designed to help gardeners with their most tedious chore: keeping weeds out of flower beds. The fabric may be plastic sheeting with perforated holes, or sheets of woven or nonwoven synthetic fibers that let air and moisture pass through. The fabric is laid over a garden bed and an opening is cut through it at each plant location. A bed of mulch on top of the fabric secures it in place and conceals it.

The fabric lets water, air, and fertilizer get through to the plant roots but blocks the growth of weeds because light cannot get through the black fabric. Unlike black plastic it lets the soil breathe and resists tearing and punctures from sharp lawn tools.

Landscape fabric also helps control erosion. It retains the soil in the garden bed by shedding excess rain water. This is especially helpful when growing plants on slopes.

Landscape fabric has been used by landscape

contractors for several years because it solves other problems. It is laid down on the ground and covered with gravel under decks to curb weed growth. And it is frequently used as an underlayment for a brick walkway or patio laid in sand or gravel. It checks weed growth and reduces heaving and settling by separating the soil and sand layers. It is also used behind retaining walls to allow drainage and reduce erosion.

Installing the fabric is easy, the only thing to watch out for is opening the large roll on a windy day. Large pieces of landscape fabric can be difficult to hold in place in very windy conditions. Wait for a calm day or at least a day with a gentle breeze.

❧ Landscape Fabric in a Bed of Flowers

Install the fabric in a garden bed that's been weeded and is free of any unwanted vegetation. Begin by measuring the garden bed and choose a roll of fabric that closely fits the dimensions. You can cut the fabric easily with a pair of scissors or a utility knife, so that's the only tool required. Where two pieces of fabric meet, overlap the edges 3 to 4 inches.

Unroll the fabric over the flower bed loosely and note where you'll need to make cuts for plant openings. The bumps make it easy to see and your cut doesn't have to be exact. Make an X slit over the plant and then gently work the fabric down to the ground. Custom-fit the fabric around each plant by making additional slits where necessary. The opening should be loose, not tight around the plant base.

Cover the fabric with 4 inches of mulch or crushed stone, spreading the layer evenly throughout the flower bed. Add new mulch as needed and make certain that all the fabric is covered, because it can break down with continued exposure to the sun.

You can use the fabric vertically to help curb weed growth between a garden bed and its timber edging material. Cut the fabric to the height of the soil, lay it up against the edging material, and backfill with soil. Make sure the soil is compact and that you have created a weed-free edging barrier.

❧ Landscape Fabric as Underlayment

If you are building a deck or are using concrete stepping stones, flagstone, aggregate blocks, or bricks for a patio or walkway, use this fabric to block out weeds and help level the soil. Lay down the fabric on top of the soil before the deck is put in place. Spread a layer of gravel on top of the fabric and you won't have to worry about pesky weeds poking through the deck boards. The fabric also eliminates water puddling and unpleasant odors caused by algae buildup in the ground below.

Landscape fabric solves an age-old problem with masonry units that heave and settle when there are changes in the ground temperature. Begin by freeing the area of weeds and grass. Make sure the area is level before laying down fabric and cut to fit as an underlayment. Cover it with a minimum of 4 inches of compacted sand. Then add a second layer of fabric and a second layer of sand. Put the masonry pieces in place and use a push broom to sweep sand into the openings between them.

WATERING AND IRRIGATION

*H*ow well your soil holds water is what determines how often watering is required. In general sandy soils require more frequent watering than clay soils because sand is porous and lets water flow through it while soils with clay retain moisture. The texture of soil is one factor affecting watering, but so is the frequency of your rainfall.

Proper watering encourages deep root growth that helps anchor a plant into the soil and keep it healthy and strong. As a rule of thumb, you can figure that your lawn or garden needs at least one inch of water a week. A nice long, gentle soaking rainfall is a gardener's delight because there's a steady supply of rainwater and time for it to seep deep down into the roots in the soil. When you use a hose, water your garden in the same way. A sporadic short burst from the garden hose encourages shallow root growth.

You have no control over the rainfall, but you can initiate watering routines to keep your lawn and garden well tended. The best time to water is early or late in the day when the temperatures and wind tend to be the lowest. Cooler temperatures and calm winds reduce the amount of water that will evaporate into the air during watering. If you live in an area where water use is restricted, contact your water department to find out if there are garden or lawn watering restrictions.

✌ When Do Plants Need Watering?

Some of the telltale signs that plants need water are leaves that curl or crinkle up, or dry leaves that turn brown and begin to drop off. Another indication that a plant is stressed and needs water is when new growth begins to wilt.

Grass is dry and wants water when you can see footprints on it. Another way to check is to dig down below the sod with a hand trowel and see if the root area is moist. If it's crusty or hard, the grass needs water. Remember not all areas of lawn require the same amount of water. Sun-drenched expanses or those affected by drying winds will need more water than those areas tucked away in the shade.

Getting water to your plants and lawn on a regular basis can be accomplished in several ways.

HOMEMADE RAIN / WATER GAUGES

SOAKER HOSE

You can use a garden hose and oscillating sprinkler, a soaker hose, or a drip irrigation system. Of course, you can drag your hose around to individual plant beds and areas of the lawn and use a spray attachment to sprinkle spot areas, but a more effective way is to know how much water your garden or lawn requires and then follow a schedule that provides just the right amount.

In general, a lawn and garden need 1 inch of water at each application. To find out how long it takes a sprinkler to deliver that much, make rain gauges. Get three plastic gallon milk bottles and cut off the tops where the bodies are widest.

Draw lines with a waterproof marker on the bottles' sides 1 inch up from the bottom. Place the gauges in the path of the sprinkler, turn the sprinkler on, and note the time. Check the water level often and when it reaches the one-inch mark in the last container, figure out how long it took. Make that your standard watering time.

❧ Equipment for Watering

You'll get the best water economy with a fixed-head sprinkler. An oscillating or rotating sprinkler wastes water. Often you can't avoid positioning a moving sprinkler without hitting pavement or walkways that don't need water, and much of the water evaporates in the air, before it reaches the soil. You can make your sprinkler more accountable by using a regulator that attaches to the hose and provides a readout of the water being used. This is a handy device when calculating water consumption.

A soaker hose is much more efficient at putting water where you want it. A soaker is a hose with holes in it. You lay it on the ground or bury it a few inches beneath the soil and connect one end to your garden hose. It brings moisture directly to the roots of the plants, where it is needed.

For watering specific areas such as around the base of a tree or bush, there are special soaker hoses that wrap around for uniform coverage. They also attach to your garden hose, and have their own on–off controls so they can be moved without leaking.

The epitome in garden watering is a drip irrigation system, which has a network of hoses, spray heads, and emitters, to automatically water plants at their roots and spray a fine mist over them at predetermined times. You customize the installation according to the size of your garden and the frequency of watering needed. While the investment isn't trivial, the long-term advantages are that you'll spend less money on water because you'll use less of it, and because watering is automatic your plants are likely to thrive.

For more about soakers, see the following pages. Also see the soaker hose project in section 3 for a do-it-yourself solution to your watering needs.

INSTALLING A SOAKER SYSTEM

*I*nstalling a soaker hose watering system in a yard is a worthwhile project. Here's what's involved. The system, consisting of hose with tiny weep holes and various fittings, is designed to be laid directly on the ground, tucked beneath a layer of mulch, or placed below ground so water can slowly seep into the roots of flowering plants, bushes, shrubbery, and vegetables.

The chief advantage of a soaker system is that it supplies water at a steady, slow rate that keeps the soil moist. No water is lost to evaporation or runoff, so the system delivers more water to the roots of plants where it's needed. You'll use less water in the long run and consequently pay lower water bills. With steady watering the plant roots stay moist but not waterlogged, so you eliminate root shock caused by normal wet–dry watering cycles. And of course you'll be free of the routine of dragging out your hose and sprinkler.

Obviously aboveground installation is easiest and can be reconfigured and moved whenever necessary. This is also true for soaker hoses laid

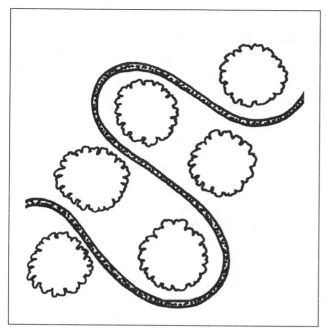

SOAKER HOSE LAID THROUGH GARDEN PLANTS

SOAKER HOSE WOVEN THROUGH HEDGE

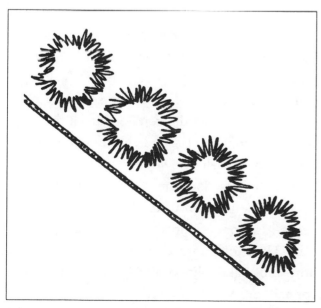

SOAKER HOSE LAID ALONG FOUNDATION PLANTING

beneath mulch. However, underground installation gives you the most watering benefits because it doesn't lose water due to evaporation and it is more permanent. If you are laying out a new garden, an underground installation is worth considering because you'll enjoy its benefits for years to come.

The typical system consists of soaker hoses attached to each other with plastic tees, elbows, and couplings. Unattached ends are capped off. Regular garden hose is used to join sections of soaker hose through areas not needing water. The system can be run under a walkway or pavement with rigid plastic pipe. The materials are

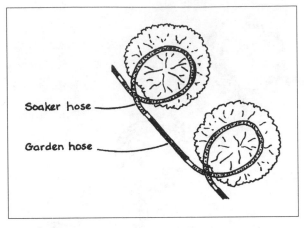

LINKING SOAKER HOSES

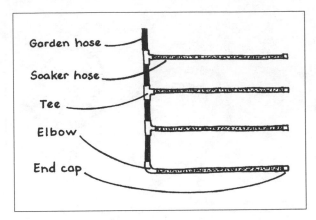

CONNECTIONS FOR PARALLEL RUNS

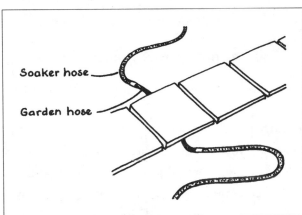

RUNNING SOAKER HOSE UNDER WALKWAY

designed for do-it-yourself installation: the hose can be cut to size with a pair of scissors, and the fittings twist on easily.

Before you shop for a soaker hose system, make a rough sketch of your yard and house, noting the location of the exterior hose spigot.

Jot down the distances from the spigot to the garden beds and the overall width and length of your property. Sketch in any new plantings you plan to add so watering them will be incorporated in your plan.

After you have your yard plan drawn, go to a home or garden center and look at the various watering systems. Take your yard sketch along so you can refer to it. Manufacturers provide planning kits that list all the components in their systems. Pick some up to research the systems; when you decide which one you'll buy, use the kit to lay out the hose locations around your yard.

Draw the location of the hose and the fittings needed to connect up the system on your yard plan. Then total up the number of feet of soaker hose and make a list of the fittings you need to connect everything together.

The hose and components are sold in kits or as

individual components. For example, you'll find water system kits with various lengths of soaker hose ranging upward from 50 feet along with all the fittings, end caps, and other components required. Purchase a kit that contains the total length of hose needed for your project. As you install the system cut off lengths of hose needed to fit your layout.

When you have all the parts together lay them out on the ground and begin assembling your system. Spend time concealing the hose by burying it under a covering of mulch or wrapping it loosely around the base of shrubbery. You can also dig a shallow ditch, place the hose in it, and cover it with dirt or mulch. Connect everything except the end caps that seal off the ends of the soaker hoses.

Hook your system to the yard faucet and let the water run full force for several minutes to flush the hose and system. Then turn the water off and install the end caps at the ends of the soaker hose. Turn the water back on and let it run while you check for leaks at the fittings. You can then adjust the water flow from the house to provide the recommended flow rate through the system. These systems have pressure regulators or simple flow restrictors that you insert in the hose to regulate the water flow.

❧ Tips for Better Installation
• Use a backflow preventer, also known as a one-way or check valve, so dirty water can't back up into your household drinking water supply. This is required by most local codes. The valve must be installed between the spigot and the first length of soaker. Make sure the arrow on the valve points in the direction of the water flow (away from the house).
• Install a filter in the system to prevent sediment and dirt particles from clogging the soaker hose.
• Keep the length of the soaker hose runs to less than 100 feet.
• Install the soaker hose 2 to 3 inches from sidewalks and other hard surfaces, which tend to absorb heat from the sun and warm the soil, reducing the spread of water.
• Bury the soaker at least 6 to 8 inches if you plan to use a rotary tiller to cultivate your garden, so the tiller doesn't chew up the soaker hose.

PROTECTION AGAINST PESTS

Common sense tells you that if your vegetable plants are being consumed by insects you must get rid of them before the plants are destroyed. There are entire books about the battle to rid fields and gardens of predators. Here, we give you the basics of protecting your plants from

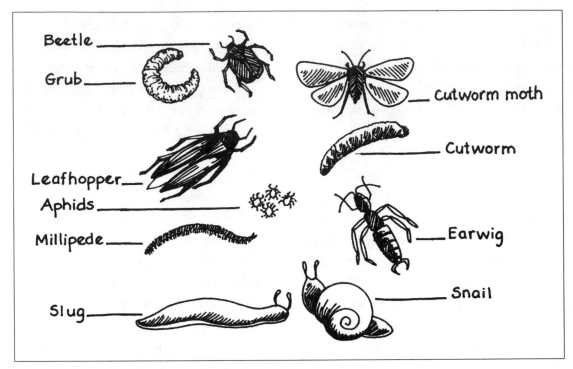

SOIL–BORNE GARDEN PESTS

pests. The goal is pretty obvious: Remove the unwanted pests and prevent them from returning.

The illustration shows some of the most common pests you'll discover. In general, garden pests damage plants by nibbling and chewing leaves, stems, and roots and sucking out plant juices. A damaged plant is less resistant to disease and drought so it is less likely to thrive.

Within a garden's ecosystem there are beneficial insects like ladybugs that enrich the soil, and unwanted insects that do nothing but prey on and destroy plant life. Let's deal with the destructive types first.

❧ Getting Rid of Unwanted Bugs

You can remove the bugs that are damaging your plants by various methods. Hand-picking them off is effective, but can be tedious and time consuming, not to mention unpleasant for the squeamish. Another tack is to put an old towel or rag around the base of a plant and shake the stems and leaves so the bugs drop onto the rag. Or spray the plant with a garden hose to wash the bugs onto the towel. Either way, don't let the bugs go free. Drop the towel into a bucket of soapy water, which will kill them.

If the pests are rampant and they cover your plants, you might need to use a synthetic pesticide such as Sevin®, or a plant-derived poison like rotenone or pyrethrum. These are available in liquid or powder form and should be applied to the infected plants sparingly. To apply a powder or dust pesticide use a hand-held or pump-type dust applicator, also called a duster. The hand-held version has a tube with a flat end and a hopper with a crank that you turn to disperse the dust. The pump-type duster looks like a bicycle pump and is useful for spraying the undersides of leaves.

The directions for using pesticides are always extensive, and unfortunately printed in small type, but read them completely before starting. Always follow the instructions carefully and to the letter.

Insecticidal soaps, which contain fatty acids that kill harmful insects on contact, are another weapon against garden pests. Some must be mixed with water, others come ready to apply in a pump sprayer bottle. Individual products will specify which pests they control, a suggested frequency of application, and where to apply, such as directly on the insect or on the underside of leaves.

When spraying or dusting on any pesticide, be careful of plants downwind that might also be affected. Apply pesticides when there is little or no wind so there is no chance of overspray. Often that's in early morning or at dusk.

An Ounce of Prevention

You can prevent a lot of insect damage by keeping your yard and garden clean and well-maintained. Pull weeds when they sprout, and don't let diseased or dead plants lie on the ground. Pick up fallen blossoms, vegetables, and rotting plant parts; these can be a breeding ground for grubs and aphids.

Keep a lookout for damaging insects. At the first sight, take action. It is not always easy to see the pests themselves; often the first alert is a damaged or chewed leaf or discolored plant. Keep a close watch and inspect your plants frequently.

If your plant is infested with an unknown insect, capture one in a jar and take it to your local county extension office for identification. Or take it to your local nursery or garden center where someone can probably tell you what it is and what you need to attack it.

Using Bugs to Get Bugs

You can use beneficial insects and organisms in your soil to ward off bad bugs. This approach is an excellent alternative to using synthetic chemical pesticides. Nematodes are naturally-occurring microscopic organisms that attack soil insect larvae. They are a natural parasite of insects and will kill insects that feed on the roots of plants. Nematodes are harmless to plants, humans, animals, birds, and beneficial insects. They carry a symbiotic bacterium into a host insect and release it. The host dies and another nematode breeds there and then leaves to find other insect hosts. Bio-Safe® is one commercial nematode product. Its new water-dispersible granule formulation is easy to use. Mix the granules with water and apply the solution with a hose-end sprayer. The treated soil should be moist when the application is made, and should be lightly watered after the application. Then water every 3 to 4 days if rainfall doesn't occur.

LAWN CARE

Just as good eating habits and regular exercise help keep us healthy, proper feeding and care will keep your lawn healthy.

How is your lawn doing at the moment? Take a walk around and check its overall appearance. Are some areas doing better than others? You might find that thick, healthy turf in the front yard turns into less healthy or weed-filled areas along the side of the house. Perhaps there's a spot where grass never grows no matter how much fertilizer and seed you lay down. Or you might find moss where grass never seems to grow on the north side of the house in a damp area shaded by a large tree. Part of your lawn that is choked with weeds might be downwind of a vacant lot that's filled with overgrowth and weeds. The point is, there is an identifiable reason for the success or failure of your lawn in each area. Much depends on where the grass is, how much sunlight it gets, and the amount of water and nutrients it receives.

❧ Getting a Lawn in Shape and Maintaining It

In early spring when the ground is dry, give the lawn a thorough raking to remove leaves, twigs and sticks, and other dropping such as pine cones and needles. Then give it a second, vigorous raking to aerate the soil or break up any dead or matted grass and increase the supply of oxygen to the grass roots.

Proper care depends on the kind of grass you have. If you don't know, take a sample to a local nursery or lawn center and ask them to identify it. If you are planting a new lawn with seed refer to the package for the best height to cut it. For new sod, ask the manager at the sod farm or garden center what the proper mowing height is. For example, tall fescues and Kentucky blue grasses are cool season growing grasses with deep root systems; they require less water than some other types and should be cut to $2\frac{1}{2}$ inches. Zoysia grass is a warm-season grass that should be cut shorter.

To give the lawn a good cut make sure your

mower blade is sharp. A sharp blade cuts evenly and does not tear off the tops of the grass blades. Don't mow wet grass because the blades of grass will stick to the blade and be torn instead of sharply cut.

If the lawn has been untended and it has grown tall trim it down to its proper height in several different mowings. The rule of thumb is to cut no more than one third of the grass height at any one time. Adjust the mower blade high for the first cutting, then lower the blade for another pass. Save the clippings to shred and use as mulch but don't let heavy layers of grass clippings lie on the lawn. Remove them and use in a compost pile. If you're just giving the grass a light trim, let the clippings stay on the lawn and decompose naturally to enrich the soil.

If you have to purchase a lawnmower, choose a "mulching mower" that cuts and chops the blades of grass and then blows the finely chopped clippings back into the lawn. If you already own a mower retrofit it with a mulching blade that converts it into a mulching mower.

Feed the lawn with a slow-release organic fertilizer that lasts for several months. Apply granular fertilizer with a hand-held broadcaster or use a push-type drop spreader; follow the application instructions given by the fertilizer manufacturer.

Fertilize cool-season grasses early in the spring, at the beginning of their growing season, and late in the fall. Warm-season grasses grow in the summer and then go dormant in cool weather; fertilize these grasses in the summer while they are growing.

❧ Dealing with Problem Areas

Sometimes you'll have to single out a trouble spot and work to improve it. The most common lawn problem areas are patches of weeds and bare spots. Remove individual weeds by hand, making sure to get the entire root. Where weeds are dense use a garden fork to churn the soil and pick the weeds out. Another alternative is to apply a grass and weed killer such as Roundup®. When the weeds have withered remove them and their roots from the soil. You'll be left with a bare spot that needs filling. If it's a small area use grass seed. If the area is large, consider filling it in with sod. That gives you the quickest results. To learn about seeding and sodding a lawn see pages 66–69.

HOW TO PRUNE HEDGES AND SHRUBS

A hedge is a group of closely planted shrubs or bushes. It can be a short dividing wall of greenery or an expansive spread across a field. Hedges are usually trimmed at heights of be-

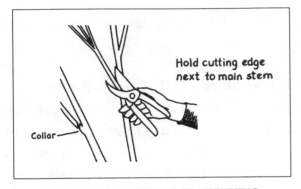

PRUNING A BRANCH FOR THINNING

Hold cutting edge next to main stem

Collar

CUTTING A BRANCH SHORT

Correct angle and distance from bud

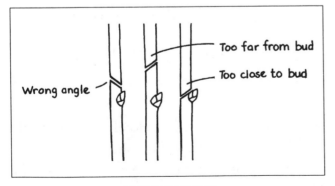

ANGLE CUTTING

Too far from bud

Too close to bud

Wrong angle

tween 3 and 6 feet to shield a house from traffic and noise. You can use plantings to form a hedge instead of building a fence or barrier between property. A line of forsythia planted between neighboring driveways, for example, creates a distinct barrier allowing privacy for both of the homeowners. A hedge of shrubs does double duty along the edge of an open field by shielding it against damaging driving wind or snowfall while adding interest to the landscape. And a hedge makes a lovely backdrop in any garden setting to showcase flower beds and decorative plantings.

Pruning a hedge or an individual shrub involves shaping, thinning, and cutting back branches with pruning shears, a pruning saw, or loppers. Use shears for branches up to $1/4$ inch in diameter, loppers for branches up to about $3/4$ inch, and a pruning or bow saw for thicker branches. Pruning shears will give a more natural looking shape.

A good pruning job is like a good haircut; no one should know you just did it. A hedge should look well manicured and groomed but not like a buzz saw just scalped it. Pruning a shrub also serves to direct its growth and increase its blossom or leaf production. When you remove some of the new buds the plant's energy is redirected to the existing buds, making them larger.

Pruning involves two basic cuts, *thinning cuts* at the collar of a branch where it originates, and *trimming cuts* that lead or head off a branch above a bud or side branch in the direction you want the branch to grow.

A hedge can be pruned to a natural or informal shape that follows its growth contour. Or it can be pruned to a formal, stylized shape, often with a deep heavy mass of growth at the base of the shrub.

Your hedge might be a row of holly bushes shielding the entrance to your back door or a long wall of privet marking your property boundary. Before you take cutting tools in hand, stand back to get an overview. Look to see how you must prune so the branches at the bottom are wider than at the top. This will ensure that sunlight and air can reach the base of the plant. If the shrubbery is a slow-growing variety you might be required to prune only a few branches, but for most shrubs you'll find more extensive pruning is required every year to maintain a uniform hedge.

Sometimes you'll find that a hedge is overgrown in one area and bare and gangling in another. The idea is to create a complete dense mass of shrubbery, so you'll need to do some selective pruning in places and some shaping and nurturing in others. In general, work from the bottom up and from the inside out. This way you clean out the old growth and allow light and sunshine to reach within the shrub.

Begin pruning by removing internal branches to break up the dense mass. At ground level remove dead growth on branches and any branches that touch the ground. Also remove shoots that are oddly shaped or ones that cross over other branches. Hold the end of the branch you're removing with one hand and the pruning tool in the other hand. Work at a comfortable distance without having to reach too far to hold the branch you're working on. Hold the cutting tool next to the main stem with the cutting blade close to and parallel with the stem.

When pruning a branch to a shorter length, cut on a slight angle about $1/4$ inch above a bud so the cut leads back to the bud or cluster of buds, which promotes more bud growth. When thinning by removing a branch entirely, cut it off at the collar where it originates. Avoid leaving a stub or making a cut flush with the main branch. Always leave a small bump or raised area where a callous will form and help heal the wound.

A rule of thumb is to prune when the plants are dormant; in cold climates that is after the first frost in the fall or before the first thaw in the spring. In warmer climates, use common sense about when to prune. Don't prune heavily in hot, dry weather with little rainfall because the shrubbery is already stressed by the unfavorable conditions.

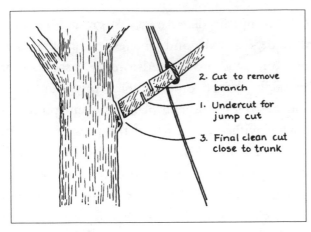

CUTTING A TREE LIMB

2. Cut to remove branch
1. Undercut for jump cut
3. Final clean cut close to trunk

PRUNING A TREE

Pruning a tree does two things: it stimulates new growth in the tree while shaping the size and direction of growth, and it removes dead and diseased branches and limbs. This rejuvenation process opens up the tree for better air circulation and exposure to the sun, both vital to its continued good health.

If you're faced with several trees that need pruning or appear diseased, consider hiring a professional tree trimmer who has both the expertise and the equipment needed. Plan to be on hand to watch the procedure and ask questions. While this is not a trivial investment you'll learn from the experience and be able to better maintain the trees yourself in the future.

Some of the specific trouble spots that pruning can correct are:

• Crossed branches that rub against each other, which creates a haven for disease
• A weak or damaged crotch (the angled area between the trunk and a branch) that will eventually split off
• An unbalanced spread of branches—too dense in one area, bare in another.

Proper pruning can correct these defects in a young tree and encourage healthy new growth. But when you're pruning an older, overgrown tree that's been neglected for years you're practicing both corrective and preventive maintenance by enhancing its shape and warding off pests and diseases.

❧ Do-it-yourself Pruning

Use a pruning or bow saw for thick branches, and loppers for branches up to ³/₄ inch in diameter. Pruning shears can usually sever branches under ¹/₄ inch in diameter. If you have a fireplace or wood stove, break up and save the branches for kindling.

Along with pruning tools you'll need a sturdy ladder for reaching the high branches of trees. If you have several trees that require pruning consider investing in a tree trimmer, also called a pole pruner. This useful specialty tool lets you reach high branches without a long ladder. The tool has a telescoping or sectional pole handle that extends its reach and a powerful lopper that you operate from the ground with a pull cord.

If overgrown branches rub against the upper story or roof edge of your house, you may be able to prune them from inside the house by working from a window. But only do that if you don't have to reach far out of the window. If you have branches that hang over gutters and downspouts plan the task of cleaning downspouts at the same time you prune off unwanted branches.

❧ Pruning Procedures

Stand back and look at the tree to decide what needs pruning and what should be left to continue growing. Take your time and walk around the tree, observing it from all sides. This is easiest when you're pruning a new tree; it has few branches and they are easy to follow from the trunk outward. Pruning an older tree that's overgrown is more challenging because it's difficult to see how all the branches are connected to the trunk.

To begin, look for dead branches devoid of leaves or signs of new growth and diseased branches that look like they're decaying. Broken live branches should also be pruned and removed so new growth can be stimulated. Prune away vertical branches that grow straight up and any crossover branches that touch other branches. Also remove sagging and bent branches.

Always keep in mind that you're trimming the tree, not severing limbs from it. The natural canopy or spread of branches around the tree should not be disturbed; instead, the branches should be thinned out and trimmed.

The basic rule of pruning is to cut at a 45-degree angle just above an outward-facing bud eye. Hold the branch slightly flexed and away from other branches so you have clear working room. Cut back a branch at the point where it meets another branch, to shorten it and let more air and light circulate around the tree. Clear away the cuttings as you work and start a pile to use as kindling.

Use a step ladder when pruning a tree. They're available in various heights up to 10 feet and provide a safe platform for reaching tree branches. Position a ladder beneath and to the side of the branch being trimmed. Extend the ladder fully with the hinges opened and the end caps seated on firm level ground. Don't stand on the top step of a ladder; it is safer to stand on a lower step and work on branches within a comfortable reach. Don't lean and extend yourself far from the ladder; it's better to move the ladder frequently so it is in close to where you're pruning.

Periodically stand back and look at the tree to observe the changes you've made. Move around the tree and view it from all sides. Remember, you can't reattach a limb once it is cut away, so work slowly and keep inspecting the tree. This will help prevent you from overpruning in one area and creating a visual hole.

To remove a large branch from a tree, make a jump cut. As illustrated, there are actually three cuts. The first two cuts cause the branch to jump or snap away from the tree trunk, then the final cut removes the stub cleanly close to the trunk. Make this kind of cut only on a tree branch that can fall unobstructed to the ground. Use the following procedure.

First saw upward from the bottom of the branch (this can be tricky) about 14 inches out from the trunk. By cutting upward first you prevent the limb from cracking and tearing the bark away at the trunk. Stop the cut when you're less than halfway through or when the saw first begins to bind in the cut. Don't continue to cut a heavy limb or it will sag and pinch the saw blade in the cut, making it difficult to remove. Then start another incision from the top of the branch a few inches out beyond the first cut. Continue cutting until the branch snaps away from the tree, leaving a stub.

Finally, cut the stub away by first making an upward incision so the bark doesn't tear as the stub falls off. Make the cut just slightly out from the tree trunk. Then cut down from the top to meet this incision.

If you have a heavy tree branch or one that hangs over a house or structure to remove consider hiring a tree expert to do the job. If there's a long, but lightweight branch that can fall directly to the ground without damaging wires or the ground beneath it, enlist the help of a friend.

Throw a rope over a sturdy branch above the one you're cutting and tie the rope around the branch you're cutting. Have a helper hold the rope or tie it to the trunk of the tree so the branch doesn't freefall to the ground when it is cut. After it is cut lower it to the ground using the rope.

A young tree with two limbs of equal size that stem from the trunk like a wishbone is a likely candidate for a weak crotch. You can prevent this from happening by shortening one of the limbs. Go about halfway up one of the limbs and cut off the top section at an outfacing bud eye. As new shoots develop the tree will be better developed.

PRUNING ROSES

The selection of roses ranges from tiny foot-high miniature plants and rose bushes (floribunda, hybrid tea, and grandiflora) to tree roses and elaborate climbers, all in a rainbow of colors, shapes, and sizes. Pruning to remove the dead canes (branches) at the base and the dead offshoots on the branches tidies up a rose plant and promotes healthy growth. You'll find that some rose plants require little in the way of pruning, but for others it's an important step that opens up the plant to more air and sunshine. By removing the dead canes you'll be able to get a better view of the lovely plant in all its splendor, reason enough for this simple, yet prickly task.

When you're working with roses it goes without saying that wearing heavy gloves is a must. Pruning roses is an easy task for an individual plant but it becomes more challenging when you have a row of overgrown rose bushes that you're trying to tame. Protect your arms and legs by wearing a long sleeve shirt and long pants. Many gardeners like the versatility of a heavy denim work apron which gives protection from prickly plants as well as has the added convenience of deep pockets for storing hand tools.

The best time to prune roses is before new growth starts in the spring. That depends on where you live; in cold-weather states plan to prune roses after the last killing frost in your area.

For climbing roses concentrate on only the dead or diseased canes until the bushes are well established, say two or three years old. Then prune sparingly to remove spindly new wood and unproductive old wood.

There's a debate over which is the best tool to use. Some rose growers prefer a sharp knife; they feel a pair of shears damages the cane because it squeezes and compresses as it makes the cut. Many other longtime rose gardeners wouldn't use anything but shears. For overgrown rose bushes with thick-diameter canes use a pair of loppers or a pruning saw.

If you have a newly planted rosebush, look for any shoots that grow from below the base of the plant. These shoots, called suckers, should be removed because they rob the plant of its strength.

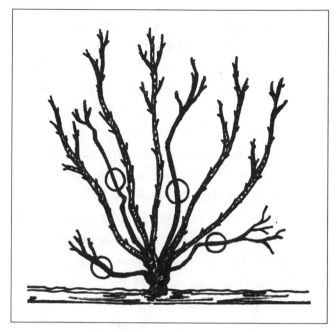

PRUNE OLDER CANES COMING UP FROM THE BOTTOM

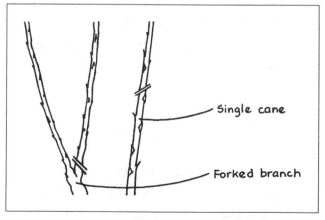

AT A FORK, PRUNE ABOVE A CANE OR BRANCH; CUT AT AN ANGLE ABOUT ¼ INCH ABOVE A DORMANT BUD FACING THE OUTSIDE

If they are growing out of the base of the plant dig down and remove the dirt around the plant so you can use a pruning saw to cut them off. If the suckers are thin remove them with a pair of shears.

Stand back and look for canes or branches that cross others and those that are damaged by winter or severe weather. As you trim away the damaged cane look carefully at its cross section. Cut away cane that is beige or brown at its center. Keep snipping down the branch until you get to the area where the cane has a white center. This is healthy wood and should not be cut further.

Where and how you make a cut is important because it determines the future growth of the rose plant. Cut at an angle about 1/4 inch above a dormant bud facing the outside. By cutting outside-facing buds you stimulate the new growth outward. This applies to pruning on a single cane or where two canes form a fork or at the base of the plant. The goal of pruning is to encourage the new growth up and outward to enhance the shape of the rose plant.

PRUNING EVERGREENS

An evergreen keeps its needles or leaves throughout the year. This property makes

evergreens a popular choice for landscaping and garden background planting because the enduring greenery makes a lovely contrast through the

PRUNING EVERGREENS

PRUNING EVERGREEN TIPS

winter months. The family of evergreens is extensive; individual types range from low-growing ground cover to stately trees. Just look around the landscape in wintertime and you'll see green leaves and needles on a surprising number of plants, such as azalea bushes, pines, and junipers. The evergreens many of us are familiar with are the needle varieties often used as foundation plantings around a house.

Pruning evergreens requires moderation. Although their shape can be severely molded, they do best when left natural, with a bit of selective nipping at branch tips to encourage new fuller growth and at the base of the plant to remove any dead or decaying branches.

Use a pruning tool appropriate to the size of the evergreen. A pair of loppers or pruning saw might be needed to cut back ungainly branches but use a pair of shears for trim cuts.

To determine the best approach to pruning an evergreen look closely at the spread of its branches. Notice how the needles or narrow leaves grow from each branch and how the branches spread out from the main leader stem in a fanlike fashion. The thin needles of a pine are long and spindly while those of a spruce are decidedly shorter. Hemlocks, yews, and firs have flat needles.

Do not cut off the main leader stem because that will have a damaging effect on how the tree shape will develop. And don't make abrupt cuts or drastically whack off branches of any ever-green; trim gradually so the plant isn't in shock because of radical pruning. Make each cut on the outside of a side bud to induce new growth next season.

As you trim away unwanted branches reach into the plant and make cuts where they will be concealed behind other branches. Don't be too heavy handed in pruning needle-bearing evergreens because they don't regenerate themselves as readily as leaf-bearing varieties. To make the plant fuller and denser remove the tip or "candle" at the end of a branch.

Some evergreens are conifers, which means they bear cones. Conifers in particular require very little in the way of pruning.

You can time pruning evergreens so the cuttings can be recycled and used as part of your holiday decorations. Keep them in a cool area with the cut stems in cold water until you're ready to use them for centerpieces or garlands. They'll remain fresh and green all through the holidays.

CARING FOR FRUIT TREES

Most popular fruit-bearing trees, such as apple and pear trees, are the prize of anyone's backyard. They are attractive to look at and

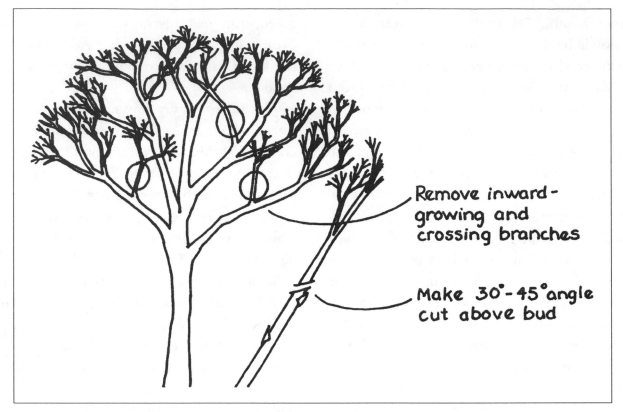

Remove inward-
growing and
crossing branches

Make 30°-45° angle
cut above bud

PRUNING FRUIT TREES

they produce fruit that can be used in a variety of ways. They like a lot of sun and room to spread their branches. Fruit trees need water and a ground layer of mulch that reaches out under the spread of the branches.

Fruit is ready to pick when you can pull it easily from the spur or short branch where it grows, which stays on the tree to produce again next season. Don't let fallen fruit sit and rot on the ground and become a breeding ground for pests and disease, rake it up and put it in a compost bin.

Pruning fruit trees does more than just make them look good, it keeps them healthy and stimulates their production of fruit. By removing branches from within the center of the tree you let the sunlight in and create a flow of air throughout all the branches.

Prune fruit trees in the spring before the sap flows, while the trees are dormant. As a tree grows and bears fruit, think of pruning as an important step to nurture the life of the tree.

To prune apple and pear trees, make each cut above an outward facing bud. As with all pruning cuts, don't go straight across the stem but angle the cut at a 30- to 45-degree angle. Thin out branches that cross over one another or those that grow inward rather than outward. Open up the inside of the tree to allow sunlight to shine on the fruit as it grows.

Look for water sprouts at the base of the tree. They usually grow straight up and look like spikes; they often grow from the site of previous pruning cuts.

If you have a dwarf fruit tree, be less ambitious in pruning it because such trees grow slowly and consequently require less trim work.

SUPPORTING PLANTS AND TREES

*M*ost low-growing plants and ground covers grow naturally without drooping over or leaning to one side, but some large flowering plants and tall vegetables need support. Strong winds and driving rain can damage these plants unless they're protected and supported so they can grow. The same is true for some young trees when they're first planted because their root systems need to get firmly entrenched in the soil. Supporting plants and trees is an easy project for a

first-time gardener and the rewards are almost immediate as you watch new growth flourish.

❧ Helping Plants Grow with Support

By bracing up large flowering plants and tall vegetables in their early growing stage they can develop "good posture" and grow to their full

SINGLE STAKE SUPPORT

MULTIPLE STAKE SUPPORT

around it and soar 4 to 5 feet high, but that's what you should allow for when laying out your vegetable garden and planning the support system.

🍂 Plant Support Systems

Some plants need a wire cage or a fence of stakes and rope, others need only an individual stake to bolster up a lengthy stem. Tall stately flowers like delphiniums, for example, can use such a brace to resist damage from strong winds and heavy rains.

When pounding a stake or support into the ground, be careful not to pierce the roots of the plant. Gently push it into the ground as far as you can, being sensitive to any resistance you might feel, then drive it with a mallet or hammer until it is firmly in place. If you hit a root, reposition the stake until you find a spot where it goes into the soil without any obstruction.

Here's a rundown of what you can use to support plants. Some supports you can make yourself, others are sold at garden centers and through mail order catalogs.

potential. All parts of a plant will enjoy air circulation, which is important to its growth. As the plant fills out, the growing foliage will cover the supports. Don't be alarmed if your little tomato plant looks like it's imprisoned in a cage or lashed to a stake; as it grows and thrives the support will be barely visible.

It's a good idea to plan ahead for support systems so there is enough space around each plant. Planning for support will help you visualize just how expansive a plant will be when it's full grown. Use the spacing information on the plant label or seed packet as a guide.

It's hard to believe that a little tomato plant will require a good 3 feet of growing space

Individual stake with tie Stakes make good plant supports. Plants can be tied to the stakes with string, plastic bag twist-ties, or scraps of fabric, rag, or any soft material. Loop the tie loosely around the plant stem so it doesn't apply pressure or cut into the stem and secure it to the stake. Position the ties every 12 inches or so.

ROPE-AND-STAKE CAGE

WIRE CAGE FOR LARGE PLANT

Cheap support materials Stakes can be made from just about any material. Here are some free or inexpensive sources.

Tree branches. The natural bark of trees blends in with the foliage of bushy plants in the garden or in containers. Use a sturdy branch at least 3/8 inch in diameter and cut it into about 3-foot lengths or to match the mature height of the plant it will support. Trim off twigs and leaves.

Recycled scrap lumber. Wood lath for plaster makes good stakes and can be found anywhere old houses are renovated. Scrap pieces of moldings and dowels are also useful as plant sup-

ports. Avoid painted wood because the paint will begin to peel and fall into the bed during the growing season as the wood weathers.

Bamboo and hardwood stakes. These are sold in home centers and come in various lengths. They are lightweight and go easily into the ground to act as a brace for plants and vegetables. You can use them to support lightweight wire mesh such as chicken wire, to hold up landscape fabric (see pages 20–22) as a protective covering for plants during cold weather, or as a trellis for growing climbing vegetables.

Old plumbing pipe. Old 1/2- and 3/4-inch galvanized water pipe makes excellent stakes for larger plants. The pipe can be cut to length with a hacksaw or pipe cutter, but you will find it much easier to have it cut to length. Pipe is a little harder to drive into the ground than thinner stakes but once in, it can support very heavy plants and fencing.

Wire mesh fencing or screening. This is good for support cages for plants. Cut the fencing material to length and secure it to stakes with a heavy-duty staple gun or with short wires twisted around the stakes and through the openings in the mesh. Form heavy-duty wire mesh into freestanding cylinders.

Prefabricated systems Prefabricated support systems come in a variety of materials and configurations. You have to shop early to get a good selection since most home and garden centers stock large amounts of these items only in the spring.

Round metal hoop supports with grids are designed for large plants like peonies. The plant grows inside the hoop and stems grow through the grid so it's barely noticeable.

Round and rectangular cages are designed for tomatoes and peppers. Look for ones with large openings between the wire so you can reach into the cage to pick the fruits of plants.

Metal and plastic-coated stake systems are sold as individual components that you assemble together. You configure them to the size needed and they link together in rectangular shapes. Be-

cause the size is not predetermined these systems work nicely for supporting large, oversize plants.

✍ Supporting a Tree

Just as tall plants and vegetables need support, a young tree often needs temporary help to get it growing straight and upright. Staking a young tree provides the support it needs to stand up against the wind while it spreads and anchors its root system firmly in the soil.

In addition to staking a tree, it helps to lightly prune or thin out some of the branches of the new tree if it is top-heavy. This reduces the

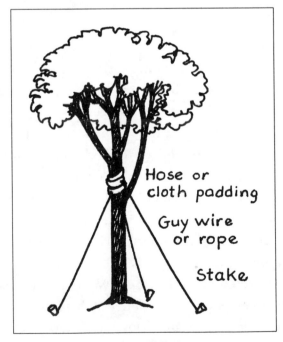

Hose or
cloth padding

Guy wire
or rope

Stake

TREE SUPPORT

weight on the trunk, cuts down wind resistance, and stimulates growth.

Trees are supported with three guy lines that run from the tree trunk to short stakes in the ground. Before positioning the stakes consider the wind pattern in your area. Locate one stake on the downwind side and the other two at angles on the upwind side. Don't pound the stakes into the root ball, instead position them about two feet beyond the ball so there's no danger of pounding into a developing root.

Trees can be supported in various ways, with a variety of materials. One way is with a tree stake kit which costs about $5 and includes three wooden stakes and support webbing. You can use

rope or wire as guy lines, but be sure to protect the tender tree trunk because these materials can chafe or cut into the bark. Run the rope or wire through short sections of old garden hose or bike tires and position the protection around the tree trunk.

PULLING WEEDS AND REMOVING STUMPS

❧ Weeds in the Grass

The best defense against weeds in a lawn is a good offense. If you maintain a thick healthy lawn, weeds won't have an opportunity to grow. It's better to cut the grass a bit long so the blades will shade the ground and retard the growth of small weeds.

A good time to weed is after a light rainfall when the lawn is soft and weeds can be eased out of the soil. Small patches of weeds can be removed by hand using a weeder. Dig the weeder into the ground under and around the weed to expose its roots. Pull the weed straight up and out of the ground removing its entire root. An oscillating hoe and bow rake come in handy to break up compact soil before removing weeds. The oscillating hoe has sharp edges and looks

PULLING WEEDS

DIGGING OUT A SMALL STUMP

something like a stirrup. Move it back and forth in the soil to dislodge weeds. A bow rake has hard teeth that dig into and break up the soil. Use these tools on the compact soil and then use the weeder to pull out individual weeds. For best results, kneel or sit on the lawn so you have good leverage. Don't leave bare spots in the lawn after you've removed weeds because that's an invitation for new weeds; add a little topsoil and grass seed. Keep a watch on the new grass patches and water them.

🪴 Weeds in Flower and Vegetable Beds

Mulching material and landscape fabrics are the first line of defense against weeds in flower and vegetable beds. Edging the beds is another way to keep the growth of unwanted weeds and grass from spreading into them.

You can cut down on the number of weeds in your garden by hand weeding or treating them with chemicals. Some are annuals and complete their life cycle in one growing season, others are perennials and send up new shoots every year. In either case the goal is to remove the weeds entirely so they can no longer flourish and germinate for another season.

🪴 Hand Weeding

Weeds can crop up in some of the darndest places, which makes extricating them by hand a challenging chore. The job will be easiest when the soil is moist—softened by rain or by a thorough sprinkling with a hose.

Ideally you want to remove a weed without the large clump of soil around its roots. To do this pull the plant straight up, instead of at an angle. The younger and smaller the weed, the easier it is to remove because its network of roots isn't firmly established in the soil.

Some weeds such as dandelions are tough critters and will regrow if only a small section of their root system is left in the ground. So when weeding, dig deep with the weeder and dig carefully to remove all parts of a weed.

Your weeding isn't complete once the weed is out of the ground. Break up the soil around the weed root system with your hand or a cultivator and look for any signs of roots or new growth and remove them. Then push the soil back into the hole and smooth it level with your hand.

A large tract of weeds can be approached with more gusto. Use a garden fork or oscillating hoe to break up the soil around the weeds and loosen their root systems before you remove them.

If you are faced with weeding a large area consider renting a rotary tiller to do the muscle work of breaking up the soil, then you can hand pick most of the weeds from the soil.

❧ Herbicides

Using chemicals to remove weeds requires a little homework. One trip to your local lawn and garden center will totally confuse you because of the vast array of weed killers. Here's the basic information you need to know. *Preplanting* herbicides are used on soil before seeds are planted; *preemergent* herbicides are used after seeding but before the seeds have germinated. *Postemergent* herbicides are used after plants have grown, and *nonselective* herbicides kill all plants they come in contact with. In the postemergent category there are *contact* herbicides, which kill only the plant tissue that they contact, and *systemic* herbicides, which are absorbed by the plant through its leaves and stem. Once inside the weed the chemicals kill the weed. They can be sprayed on or painted on the leaves of a weed with a small brush.

When using chemicals be very careful to read and follow the "Caution" information on the label. Apply all garden chemicals on a windless day or early in the morning, when the wind usually is calm. Don't apply any chemicals if there is rain in the weather forecast. For systemic herbicide or any other garden chemical or fertilizer to be effective it must remain on the plant or in the soil in order to be absorbed by the plant. Wind and rain can blow or wash the chemicals out of your lawn or garden and into the drainage system surrounding your property. Eventually these chemicals end up in the river and groundwater systems. In urban areas chemical runoff from residential lawns and gardens is a major source of pollution; the careful use and proper application of all garden chemicals will go a long way in reducing this contamination.

❧ Getting Rid of Weeds in Tough Places

Weeds in a stone or brick path or driveway can be a perennial problem. The best solution we've found is to wait for a weather forecast calling for rain and then sprinkle borax on the weeds. The rain will wash the borax into the weed and kill it. Don't get it too close to nearby plants, however.

There are a host of chemical defenses for spot control of weeds. The careful spraying of a herbicide directly on the weed quickly kills it. The containers of many spot weed killers come with a spray attachment that is very easy to use.

❧ Removing Tree and Shrubbery Stumps

Beware: stump removal is a job that requires strength and stamina. You can remove small shrubbery stumps, those less than a foot or so in diameter yourself, but it's not an easy job. You'll need sharp digging tools like a shovel, garden fork, and spade—and a strong back. Wear eye protection, gloves, and work shoes. Cutting through the root system is real work so you will find it time well spent to sharpen your shovel and other cutting tools before you begin this project. A sharp lawn edger comes in handy to cut tough roots, so do a pruning saw and a lopper.

Begin by digging around the stump with your shovel. Start about a foot away and angle the shovel blade toward the stump. As soon as you begin digging you will hit the roots of the stump. Cut through the small roots with your shovel; cut larger roots with a lopper or pruning saw. Dig toward the stump so as the hole gets deeper it tapers down to the center. You want to cut the roots but at the same time you want to dig as small a hole as possible.

Some of the most difficult roots to cut are the ones growing down out the bottom of the stump. After you have dug around the stump push it back and forth to loosen it as much as possible. Then work your shovel under the stump to cut the roots.

Pulling on the stump is sometimes difficult to do. You can rent a ratchet winch, often called a comealong, and hook it to the stump and a nearby tree. Or you can tie a rope to the stump, tie the other end to your car's bumper and have someone pull slowly and steadily on the stump while you chop away at the root system with the shovel. Don't pull too hard or you will damage your car. Be sure that the rope is in good shape and strong. Don't stand between the car and the stump because you could get hit if it comes loose suddenly or the rope breaks.

To remove stumps 12 to 24 inches or larger hire a professional or rent a stump grinder. A stump grinder is a gas-powered machine that is lowered on the stump and has a large wheel that grinds the stump into small chips. The grinder does not remove the stump, it just grinds it down to below the soil level so it is not visible.

MAKING A COMPOST PILE

When a plant dies it begins to decompose into its basic elements, adding valuable nutrients to the soil in the process. As a home gardener you can hurry this natural ocurrence along by controlling the conditions, a technique called composting. By composting your yard waste you can recoup valuable organic material. You'll also do your share to keep yard waste out of already crowded landfills. Leaves, grass, and pruning waste take many years to decompose when they are encased in plastic bags and buried in a landfill. The same material can be composted into mulch and used to nurture your plants and lawn.

The best yard waste for a compost pile is equal amounts of leaves and grass clippings. Hedge trimmings can also be added. For uniform decomposition the leaves and grass clippings should be dry and finely shredded. Run over them several times with a lawnmower or shred them in a yard shredder. You can also add food scraps like eggshells and coffee grounds to a compost mix, but avoid meat and other foods with fat, which prevent the material from breaking down and may attract rodents.

Keep the compost in a bin. One about 3 feet by 3 feet square and at least 3 feet deep is a good size for a start. This will provide room for a good size pile of compost and space where it can be mixed. Build your bin directly on the soil in either a sunny or shady area.

You can build a wooden compost bin like the one on pages 131–134, or you can stack up walls of concrete blocks with their holes facing upward. You can also use shade fencing, which is thin wooden boards bound into several rows of wire. It is sold in rolls and used to protect shrubs and delicate plantings from wind, sun, and snow.

A very simple compost bin can be made out of a piece of heavy wire mesh called hardware cloth. Rolls of mesh are 3 feet wide. Form a 10-foot

COMPOST PROVIDES COST-FREE NUTRIENTS FOR A GARDEN

length into a cylinder and tie the ends together with heavy twine. Then place the cylinder on end and fill it with your compost material. To mix it up, just lift the wire off and set it next to the pile. Then fork the pile back into the bin.

You can also purchase ready-made compost bins at most home and garden centers; they are made from recycled plastics or rot-resistant woods.

Dump waste to be composted into the bin and add water so the material feels like a damp sponge. Use a garden fork to mix the material thoroughly (this can be heavy work) to ensure that it is damp throughout. Do this every couple of days. If it rains, cover the compost pile so it doesn't become saturated with water and leach out all the nutrients into the soil beneath.

In two to three days the compost will begin to heat up and you may even see steam rising from the pile. This is good, for it signals that bacteria are at work decomposing the material. Your compost should reach about 160 degrees in the center.

You can use a metal coat hanger as a probe to get an idea of how hot it is. Straighten out the hanger and push it into the center of the pile. Let it sit for a few minutes and then pull it out. The wire will feel warm to the touch if your pile is really working well. In the summer be careful because the wire can get too hot to touch.

In about three weeks the material should appear to be dark and crumbly and smell earthy. If it begins to smell unpleasant it needs to be turned over more frequently to get more oxygen beneath the surface.

GETTING AN OVERGROWN YARD IN SHAPE

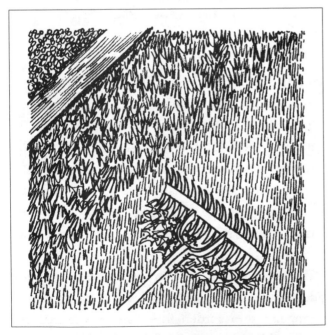

TENDING AN OVERGROWN YARD

*I*f you have a house with Neglected Yard Syndrome there's a simple remedy. Resist the temptation to go through the yard with a chain saw and electric hedge clippers, whacking down anything and everything. It is far better to take a slow but steady course of action that lets you first trim back ungainly overgrowth and then discover what's worth keeping and what's not.

If possible, see how the landscaping elements work during the four seasons before making any major adjustments. Maybe the old maple you want to remove does a fine job of shielding the patio from the hot summer sun. You won't know that until you've seen how the sun affects the area, and the temperature inside the house. Maybe you should wait before ripping out the massive hedge that separates your house from the neighbors. It might be there for a reason, like quelling the noise from their Labrador retriever. Before you make major changes to the landscape, wait until you've lived a year in a house.

In the meantime, there is a great deal you can do. You can take a slow and steady approach to taming a yard that has grown out of control. Not knowing where to start and what strategy to follow can seem overwhelming, so here's a game plan with advice about how to do it.

❧ Step One

Nothing helps improve the look of your yard like a well-mowed lawn. First pick up fallen tree branches and break them up to use for kindling; the older and dryer they are, the better for starting fires. Stack them like firewood or store them in an old barrel or bin.

If there are heavy layers of dried leaves, rake them up. If your community has a lawn refuse program, find out how to have the leaves removed or where to take them for disposal. Otherwise, you can bag them for garbage pick up or start a pile for composting. Shredded dry leaves are a good source of mulch, so it's worth saving some if you have the space.

Mow the lawn; depending on how long it is you may have to mow it more than once. Shred the grass clippings with the lawnmower and save

them for mulch or the compost bin. Rake up any heavy clumps. Use a thatching rake to remove clumps of dead and dried grass roots in the lawn and reseed any bare spots. (For specific lawn care and mowing information see pp. 30–31.)

❧ Step Two

Move on to the flower beds and foundation plantings around your house. Rake out any leaves and remove sticks and debris in these areas. The length of time this will take depends on the size of your yard and what shape it is in. Yard clean-up work pays off when you discover plants and shrubs or details you didn't know were there, like an old brick edging long overgrown with ivy or the hint of an old strawberry patch.

❧ Step Three

Stroll around the yard and make a rough sketch that pinpoints where trees, shrubbery, and other objects are located in relation to the house. Mark where paths run through the yard and where fencing and gates are located. The sketch will provide a useful view of the yard as a whole and allow you to focus on individual components or work areas.

❧ Step Four

For a quick burst of color to make a first impression at the front door, fill containers with bright red petunias or other colorful fast-growing annuals. If there are window boxes, fill them with a bounty of colorful blooms. These are low-cost improvements and an easy way to beautify your home.

Step Five

Separate the yard into work areas such as the foundation plantings and shrubbery in the front yard, the side yard and driveway, and the deck and foundation plantings at the rear of the house. Concentrate your efforts on taming the jungle of overgrown shrubs and weeds in one area at a time. One strategy to maximize the "curb appeal" of your house is to start at the front and work your way to the rear. Another approach, if you have little ones confined to playing in the backyard, is to start there, for immediate benefits from your labor. Or let practicality decide where you'll begin. If you can't get your car in the driveway alongside your house because a row of overgrown lilac bushes is in the way, that's a good place to start your yard work.

Step Six

Wherever you're working, the mission is to gain control of what's there. Pull out weeds and remove any dead stumps. Cut back all the dead, diseased, and broken branches at the base of overgrown shrubbery. Then stand back and look at the shrubs to do some selective pruning to get them back in shape. (See "How to Prune Hedges and Shrubs," pages 31–33 for more details.) A real nuisance in overgrown gardens are stump sprouts, which are spindly shoots at the base of trees. Saw them off wherever you see them.

Step Seven

If you're faced with a row of hearty shrubs like forsythia that are beyond pruning, cut them down to their base; you should find that they grow right back next season. But since not all plants are tough enough to withstand such drastic cutting, ask for advice at your local nursery.

Step Eight

The physical part of your work is over and now the fun begins. Plant a combination of annuals and perennials to give you a combination of instant color and long-term interest and variety in your garden.

FALL AND WINTER CHECKLIST

There's a great sense of accomplishment to be found in cleaning up a backyard on a crisp fall afternoon. With the sun on your back and brisk fall breezes spurring you on, the weather conditions are ideal for completing yard chores.

Getting a backyard ready for a winter rest basically involves cleaning up the lawn and garden and building up the soil so it is fertile for planting next season.

❧ Cleanup

Begin your cleanup by dealing with fallen leaves. Run your lawnmower over them with a collector bag, and then add them to your compost bin or use them as mulch around trees and shrubbery. If you're inundated with leaves and have too many to handle, find out if your local recycling center has a pickup day. Leaves collected in plastic bags crowd landfill areas, so finding a way to recycle them is good for everyone.

Rake up pine needles separately to use as mulch in beds. And collect pinecones, gum balls, or any other droppings from Mother Nature. You can use them in decorating projects or give them away to craftspeople, who consider them a bounty.

Remove any wilted and spent plants in the garden because they don't break down and decompose easily. Pull out annuals and trim back dead leaves and stems from perennials. Take out plant supports and stakes so the garden can be hand-raked to remove debris and leaves. A small hand-held cultivator works well to rake within the confines of flower beds. And while you're at it, pull out any weeds that you find.

Take a walk around your house to see where the foundation plantings need tidying-up. Often you'll find scattered papers and leaves tangled in the underbrush. When all the soil is raked clean, use mulch to cover the base of the shrubs.

This is a good time to give a light pruning to trees that have shed their leaves, because you have a good look at the shape of the branches. Now is the time to remove misdirected and dead branches.

It is also a good time to prune other trees and shrubs. For more information about that see pages 31–41.

Reposition any edging material like brick or timbers along garden beds, patios, and walks that might have gotten moved or mislaid.

❧ Building Up the Soil

Making a soil rich with nutrients is like making a good soup. It takes lots of ingredients and plenty of time to stew. Fall is the ideal time to add slow-releasing organic fertilizers so all winter long the soil is enriched and improved. Add peat moss to improve the nitrogen level and amend the soil with composting materials. Work everything together. If the area is small use a hand cultivator to mix the fertilizer and compost into the soil. For larger areas lightly rake the soil and crush up the lumps. Then add amendments and use a rake or fork to mix them all together with the soil.

When all the cleanup work is done and the soil is bursting with fertility it's time to plant early-flowering bulbs to welcome in the new season. See pages 72–75 for information about planting bulbs.

❧ Attracting Birds

Don't forget to fill a bird feeder for hungry feathered visitors who frequent your yard during the winter months. Set out a source of water for them, too. Attracting birds to your yard all year round is a good idea. During the growing season they thrive on insect and aphid eggs, caterpillars, grubs, and beetles, to mention just a few of a gardener's enemies, but in the winter they need your help.

❧ Winter Watch

If you have a heavy snowfall that settles on evergreens and shrubs, remove the snow before it becomes encrusted and too heavy for the plant to support. Use a broom to gently sweep off the snow or shake the branches to dislodge it.

SECTION II

Easy Planting Methods and Projects

PLANTING BASICS

When you plant a tree or a flower or a vegetable you're putting it in a new environment; that is, you're moving a living thing from the shelter of its container into foreign territory. You want to make the transition for the plant as simple and stress-free as possible.

How Many Plants Do You Need?

The National Garden Bureau suggests a formula to calculate the number of plants needed to fill an area:

1. Measure the width and length of your garden in feet and calculate its area in square feet (width × length = square feet). If the area is irregularly shaped—oval, round, or long and winding—a rough estimate is good enough. Make straight-line measurements that box in the area.

2. Use this table below to estimate the number of plants you need.

RECOMMENDED SPACING, IN INCHES	NUMBER OF PLANTS PER SQUARE FOOT
6	4.00
8	2.25
10	1.44
12	0.44
24	0.25

Example: A garden measures 10 feet by 12 feet 6 inches; its area is 10 × 12.5 = 125 square feet. You want to put in plants that require 10-inch spacing. From the table, that is 1.44 plants per square foot. So you need 125 × 1.44 = 180 plants. You should get a few more, in case some are damaged by weather, animals, or pests. If you will use plants with different spacing recommendations, estimate the square footage you will devote to each type and use the table to calculate the number of plants that will fit in each area.

When to Plant Depends on Where You Live

The ideal time to plant is when the soil and air temperature are warm enough to nurture and support plant life. To find out when the danger of frost in your area has passed talk to neighbors who are gardeners and ask at your local nursery or garden center.

The following illustration on page 58 is adapted from a Plant Hardiness Zone Map published by the United States Department of Agri-

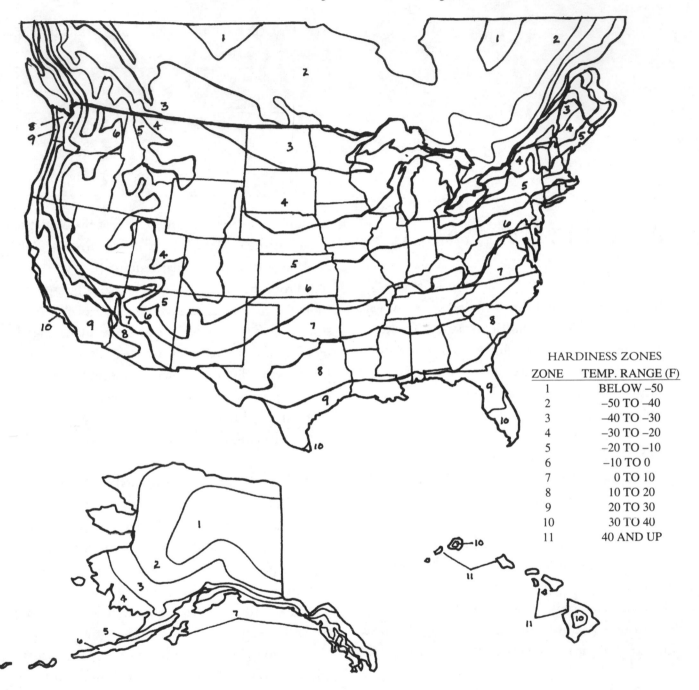

HARDINESS ZONES

ZONE	TEMP. RANGE (F)
1	BELOW −50
2	−50 TO −40
3	−40 TO −30
4	−30 TO −20
5	−20 TO −10
6	−10 TO 0
7	0 TO 10
8	10 TO 20
9	20 TO 30
10	30 TO 40
11	40 AND UP

HARDINESS ZONES

culture (USDA) and used by home gardeners and commercial nurseries to determine when plants should be shipped to different parts of the country so they will survive if planted on receipt.

Learn what zone you live in. You'll use the information often, especially if you order from gardening catalogs because mail-order plants are often catalogued by the zones in which they can survive and thrive.

❧ Hardening Off

If you bring plants home before you can plant them, acclimate them to their new environment. Keep them moist and protected from strong winds. Move them out into the full sun slowly so they'll adjust to their new surroundings. The process is similar to bringing new seedlings sown indoors to the outside; it is called *hardening off*. By introducing plants to their new environment gradually you will give them a chance to toughen up so they will have the strength to ward off pests and withstand the elements once outside.

To prepare a site for planting, cultivate the soil so it is loose and granular and crumbles in your hand. Use a garden fork and a hoe or shovel to loosen the soil and dislodge large clumps. Remove any old roots, shells, or other debris. To break up large clods in the soil use a stirrup hoe or hand cultivator. If you're adding fertilizer or compost now is the time to mix it in, as you turn over the soil.

❧ Planting

Water the plants a few hours before transplanting them so they will slide easily out of their containers. Pinch off any open blooms and snip off any withered leaves. Position the plants by arranging them on the soil, making sure that you allow plenty of growing room around them. When you're pleased with the arrangement, put the plants off to one side and dig holes for them. Dig the holes for small plants with a trowel; use a shovel for larger holes. The hole should be larger than the container holding the plant. If you're adding plant food, do it at this time.

Carefully remove the plant from its container by gently squeezing the sides of the container to dislodge the soil. If it refuses to come out tap the container sharply against a hard surface like a fence post or the flat side of a shovel to loosen the dirt. If the plants are small and contained in plastic trays, pop the individual plants out by pressing on the bottom of the tray.

Handle the plants with care, holding them by the ball of soil and root. Poke a few holes in the sides of the soil around the root to open it up a little. Place the plant into the hole and fill in the soil around it. Make sure that you don't bury the plant too deeply, or too shallowly so that the root ball sticks out of the ground. Try to set the plant at the same depth that it was in the container. Level the soil around it and cover with a layer of mulch for protection and to conserve moisture.

SOME HERBS GROWN INDOORS

GROW HERBS INDOORS

There's nothing more enticing and delicious than adding zest and flavor to a recipe with freshly grown herbs. Quick cooks can spruce up canned soups and entree with a sprig of parsley or chives. And the aroma of fresh herbs in a kitchen can't be matched by any synthetic room freshener. In the winter those tastes and smells are even more welcome.

To bring herbs indoors, plant them in containers and set them on a window sill or on a table in front of a sunny window. Those same containers can go outside when weather permits to sit in a nice grouping on a porch or patio.

Some herbs that grow well in containers indoors are parsley, thyme, bush basil, dill, and chives. These are all pretty popular additions to recipes and they're easy to grow.

❧ Windowsill Garden

If you have a sunny window that gets a good five hours of sunlight everyday during the winter you have an ideal spot for growing herbs. Make sure that the window is well insulated and not drafty, because cold chills can damage plants.

❧ Minigreenhouse

If you don't have a sunny window location for an indoor herb garden, use "grow light" fluorescent tubes. They are available in lengths from 18 to 48 inches. Hang the fixture 10 to 12 inches above a table full of plants or seedlings. Turn the lights on 12 to 14 hours a day and the plants in your makeshift greenhouse will grow contentedly.

❧ Seeds or Seedlings

You can sow herbs from seed or buy seedling transplants. To sow from seed follow the directions in the next project. However, for your first adventure in growing herbs indoors we suggest starting with seedling transplants, which are sold as individual plants in containers at garden centers and nurseries.

Planting Use a potting soil mixture that contains ingredients like vermiculite and organic material such as peat moss. This is lighter than conventional potting soil and very convenient to use. You'll find it in large home centers, garden centers, and nurseries. Also pick up some fish emulsion or liquid plant food to feed the herbs about once a month.

Plant herbs in containers that have drainage holes in the bottom and place the containers on a tray or saucer. It is important that water can drain from the container, so it isn't trapped in the soil where it can rot out the root system. Fill the container halfway with potting mix and then gently remove the herb from its container. Inspect the plant and remove any dried leaves. Poke a few holes with your finger in the soil around the roots and then position the plant in the container. Make sure that it is upright and centered if it is in an individual container. If the herb is part of a grouping make sure that there's plenty of growing room for all the plants. Fill the container with more potting mix, packing it gently around the plant. See that the soil in the container is level with the top of the root ball.

Care and feeding   Water the herb whenever necessary. To find out, poke a finger into the soil. If it comes out dry, the plant needs water; if not, wait a day or two and check again. You can use a long-necked watering can to add water to the soil and to the tray so water is absorbed up from the plant roots. Another way to water a plant is to place its container in a sink of water so the water

can be absorbed up through the roots. Let the excess water drain off before returning it to the tray.

As the herbs grow you'll notice they tend to stretch toward the light. To prevent having lopsided plants, rotate them occasionally so they grow straight and full.

❧ Using Home-grown Herbs
A reminder about cooking with fresh herbs:

1 tbls. of fresh herbs = 1 tsp. dried herbs.
Dried herbs are stronger than fresh ones. Adjust your recipes accordingly and add the fresh herbs late in the cooking process so their flavor isn't weakened.

SOW SEEDS INDOORS

A first-time gardener can get a lot of enjoyment from a small investment in seeds by sowing them indoors in the late winter. The bonus comes when these young healthy seedlings are transplanted to the garden to create a bonanza of flowers and vegetables. Watching the growth from tiny sprouts to well-formed seedlings is part of the fun. Another advantage is the money you'll save. For gardeners who won't settle for run-of-the-mill plants, there's an amazing selection of varieties sold only as seed, and not available as prestarted seedlings or transplants.

You can buy seeds in many places. Certainly they're sold in large display racks in garden centers and nurseries. You'll also find seed packets in hardware and grocery stores. There are many mail-order catalogs selling seeds and planting materials and tools. Some catalogs also provide exceptional reading material. Their full-color pictures show and tell you everything you want to know about particular plants and their properties.

Don't be intimidated about sowing seeds indoors. It's a three-part process that begins with planting seeds to germinate and then transplanting the sturdiest seedlings to another container where they can grow. The final move is to transplant them outdoors in the garden, where they can reach maturity.

If you're an early-bird gardener sowing seeds indoors might be just the project for you. To know when to start, work back from when you want to plant them in the garden and when your area is free of frost.

Many seed packets list the number of days to germinate and then the number of weeks the seeds require to bloom. For example, the information on a packet of snapdragon seeds, which is a lovely annual for any garden, reads: "For earliest bloom, start in a sunny window 6 to 8 weeks before transplanting outdoors." It says the seeds will germinate in 10 to 15 days, when the stem and first leaves appear. The packet also shows a drawing of how to identify the seedling, and includes a map of the United States indicating when to plant outdoors, when there is no longer any danger of frost in the area. Use the information on the seed packets as general guidelines for starting seeds. But use your common sense and knowledge of local conditions and don't transplant seedlings outdoors too early; wait until the soil is warm and welcoming.

Some serious gardeners have elaborate greenhouses and high-tech grow-light systems (not to mention a lot of room) but you don't need an expensive setup. You can grow seeds into healthy transplants or seedlings with a few basics and a lot of tender loving care. What's important is to observe and tend to your new seedlings on a daily basis so they get off to a good start.

❧ Basic Setup

Seeds need warmth, moisture, and light to nudge them up and out of the soil. A large table in front of a sunny window is ideal; the window sill will do just fine.

The temperatures should range between 65° and 75°F, so the window should be weathertight and not allow cold drafts to seep through in the evening when the sun goes down. If there's any danger of a chill move the seedlings to a warmer spot.

Natural light from an eastern or southern exposure works well. You can add artificial light with incandescent or fluorescent grow lights hung over the seedlings. However you choose to provide light for the seeds, it's important to be able to turn the seedlings around easily so they don't grow leaning toward the light.

❧ Containers

You can use any flat container with drainage holes; for example, the black plastic nursery flat that transplants are sold in. Or you can retrofit an old plastic container such as a cat's litter box and drill holes in the bottom. Smaller trays work well too.

You can make individual containers by cutting down the sides of a plastic beverage or liquid laundry detergent container with a utility knife. Make the container about 3 inches high, which is a convenient working size. Make a few holes in its bottom with a hammer and nail or a drill, so excess water can drain out.

Smaller individual seedling pots can be made from recycled styrofoam cups, yogurt containers, or whatever is similar that you have on hand. You can also use a fiber egg carton, which can go right into the ground. The cardboard tube from inside a roll of toilet paper can be used; just cut it in half and put it directly into the soil.

You can buy individual peat and fibrous plant pots that go right into the ground. Garden centers also sell plastic compartmentalized seed cells, often called cellpacks, that you can reuse next year. Make sure these containers are clean by washing them in hot water and a little bleach and rinsing thoroughly before use.

You need a large tray or several of them to hold the containers or flats of seedlings for watering purposes. Many gardeners feel bottom watering is best for young seedlings because water seeps up through the soil evenly. If your bathtub or wash sink are nearby you can set the flat or containers in a few inches of water to absorb moisture that way, but be careful not to soak them. Other gardeners say a gentle shower from a sprinkling can with a rose spray head on the end is equally effective. Don't overwater seedlings because it can result in "damping off," a condition caused by a soil-borne fungi when seeds rot and stems shrivel up.

❧ Soil

Whatever container you choose, fill it with a seed starting soil mix or soilless seed mixture, both sold at nurseries and garden centers. Don't use ordinary soil from your garden because it's too dense and heavy, which will stifle young seedlings' growth.

Here are two formulas for making your own starting soil mix:

1. Combine 1 part milled sphagnum moss with 2 parts vermiculite and 2 parts perlite.

2. Combine equal parts of potting soil, peat moss, and vermiculite.

Instead of using soil you can buy compressed seed starter soil wafers and peat pellets. These expand in size when water is added and are easy to use for sowing seeds.

PLANTING SEEDS

COVER WITH PLASTIC TO CONSERVE MOISTURE

❧ Sowing Seeds

Pour seed starting soil into a container until it's about $1/4$ inch from the rim. Follow the directions from the seed producer and plant the seeds at the depth suggested on the package. Let the seeds fall loosely, don't pack them in. Water the soil before adding seeds. Get the soil damp but not saturated. A spray bottle is handy to use for this purpose.

Use your finger to gently poke holes in the soil or drag a pencil through the soil to create a groove. How deep you plant a seed is critical because you can bury it forever if you go too deep. In general you can figure to cover a seed with soil about three times the seed's thickness. Space the seeds so they won't be crowded next to one another. Give them room to grow.

How you actually plant the seeds depends on their size and how adept you are at handling them. Many seeds are so minuscule it's a good idea to mix them with some dry sand and gently press them into the soil without burying them. You can sprinkle seeds directly out of the packet into grooves you have cut into the soil, too.

Follow the suggestion on the seed packet for depth and spacing. A common instruction is two or three seeds in a cell or individual container. When the seeds are in place, gently tap the soil over them. Most young seedlings look alike, so identify them with a marker of some kind to tell you what they are.

🐦 Growing

Keep the seedlings warm and well lighted, and moistened with water. Humidity helps the seeds to germinate, so cover them with a sheet of clear plastic food wrap until their first set of leaves sprouts, then remove the covering. Maintain the same growing conditions. Check the moisture level by sticking your finger into the soil to see if it feels dry.

🐦 Transplanting

When the second sets of leaves sprout, it's time to prepare for the second phase of growing seeds: getting the strong and healthy seedlings potted and on their own. Fill new containers, or flats—which allow for wider spacing—about two-thirds

PLANTING FROM SEEDLINGS

full with potting soil and dampen it.

Handling these delicate little creatures can be tricky. Some gardeners insist on using tweezers, others hold the seedling by its leaf, not its stem. Gently tap the sides of the container around the seedling and lift it out with a spoon or craft stick and carefully maneuver it to the new container. If you have a cellpack, the seedling will probably slide right out if the soil is damp or require a gentle nudge from the bottom. When making the transfer, keep the seedlings out of bright lights and drafts, which can stress them.

When they're firmly settled, with new soil packed gently around their stems, give the seedlings a gentle dose of diluted fertilizer. Then keep them warm, watered, and well lighted until they are strong and the weather conditions are safe for them to move outdoors.

🐦 Hardening Off

The process called "hardening off" refers to the week or so of getting seedlings prepared for life outdoors. You put young seedlings through this initiation period by setting them outdoors for a few hours every day to toughen them up. This is what a cold frame or starter seed potting box is designed to do (see pages 135–139).

If you don't have a cold frame, place the seedlings on a protected porch or beside the house where they won't get an overdose of full sunlight or strong winds. An area that's protected from the wind, with light morning sun, is ideal. Gradually increase the time in the sun by about an hour each day as the week progresses. Of course bring the seedlings indoors at night or if there's threat of cold weather, severe rainfall, or heavy winds.

For their final coming-out party, choose an overcast day with mild temperatures and settle them in their new spots in the garden in freshly dug planting holes that have been moistened with water and enriched with organic matter. Then water them regularly so they get all the moisture they need to grow.

SEEDING AND SODDING A LAWN

To create a lawn you can grow it from seed or lay down sod. There are pros and cons for both methods. A roll of sod is more expensive initially than grass seed and requires more work to install, but it does produce an instant lawn. Seed, on the other hand, requires a continued effort to maintain and nurture a lawn to maturity. Both require considerable amounts of water. In areas where water rates are high, that can be a significant expense.

In general, warm-season grasses grow best in southern states and cool-season grasses are adapted for northern climates. Warm-season grasses grow during the summer months and cold-season grasses grow in the spring and fall when temperatures are cool. If you're uncertain about the types of grass that grow well in your area, ask at your local nursery or garden center. A knowledgeable person there can suggest not only the types of grass that do best in your area, but which type is most suitable for the conditions around your house.

❧ Preparation

This is the grueling part of creating a lawn because it's the most labor intensive. The extent of the work depends on how much property you have to seed or sod. For large areas consider renting power equipment; smaller jobs can be done using hand tools.

If you're seeding or sodding the lawn of a newly-built house you'll probably need topsoil and grading. This is a job to hire out because it involves dump truck loads of soil that must be spread evenly across the property. Check to see that the soil is graded at a slight slope away from the house so water will drain away from the foundation.

Before you begin, it is a good idea to test the soil to see if it needs amendments (see pages 13–14). For lawns, soil should have a slightly acid pH level of about 6.5. To raise the pH level add lime, to lower it add sulphur. The results of a soil test explain how much material should be added to your particular soil.

When you go to work, the milder the weather

conditions, the better. Remove any plants, rocks, roots, weeds, sod, and anything else that is taking up space where your new lawn is planned. Use a shovel, hoe, or spade to turn over the soil and pick up anything you can't remove with a rake. For a large expanse of lawn, rent a rotary tiller to help you push and move the soil around. A wheelbarrow comes in handy to haul away debris.

When the soil has been cleared, add granular nutrients and amendments as indicated in your soil test, using a drop or broadcast spreader. Give the area a final raking to break up any remaining clumps of soil and then water it to bring down the dust and work the materials into the soil so they don't blow away.

PLANT GRASS SEED WITH A BROADCAST SPREADER
IN TIGHT CORNERS AND WHERE A DROP SPREADER
CANNOT BE USED

&• Seeding a Lawn

In general, sowing 3 pounds of grass seed per 1,000 square feet will yield a nice lawn and not break your bank account. However, be sure to follow the recommendations regarding minimum coverage printed on the package of grass seed, because some grass mixtures should be sowed more densely.

Use a drop spreader to dispense grass seed over a large area; it is more accurate than a hand-held broadcast spreader. In some areas, such as in a tight corner, you may have to spread the seed by hand or use a broadcast spreader.

Use a rake to gently push the seed into the soil. Be careful not to bury the seed too deeply. Sow the seed no more than $1/4$ inch deep in the soil. Then use a lawn roller (available at a rental center) to roll the seeded area.

Next, you must protect the seed with a $1/4$-inch layer of mulch to prevent it from being blown away and to help contain moisture in the soil. Water the soil by soaking it down to a good 6 inches, then water with a fine spray mist at least once a day until the seeds germinate, which can take as long as three weeks with some types of grass. After the seeds germinate and begin to sprout you can use a standard sprinkler to water the area.

LAY SOD FOR AN INSTANT LAWN

❧ Sod

Sod is fully matured grass growing in soil that is cut into strips. It is grown on sod farms and then peeled up complete with its roots and laid on soil creating a full grown lawn. Laying down sod is often compared to installing wall-to-wall carpeting, but sod is a lot heavier and usually it covers a much larger area than carpeting.

Purchasing sod To determine how much sod is needed, measure length and width of the area and multiply them together to get the number of square feet in the new lawn. Sod is often sold in 2-foot-wide strips of various lengths. Check with the nursery or sod farm you plan to deal with to find out the exact dimensions of their rolls. Many sod rolls are 2 feet wide and 3 feet long, so each roll covers 6 square feet. If you are putting in a 1,000-square-foot lawn, you will need about 170 rolls of sod.

That much material will weigh over a ton, so don't even consider transporting it yourself. Have the sod delivered to your house, preferably just a day before you can lay it. This is especially important during hot weather because the sod rolls can dry out when left standing in the sun. If you must hold sod for two or three days, mist-spray the rolls and cover them with plastic sheeting. Water the soil thoroughly the day before you plan to lay the sod.

Laying sod Begin laying the sod along a driveway or sidewalk so you can work from a straight edge. Arrange the individual rolls end to end butting their ends together so the seam is nearly invisible. Gently press the ends together. If the sod rolls don't unroll easily and lie flat, it may be necessary to sprinkle them with water to soften the soil. This will also help the end joints go together.

After laying one row, note where the joints are so you can plan the layout of the next row. Think of the pieces of sod as if they were bricks and stagger them so the joints in one row don't line up with the joints of the preceding row. You can easily cut a sod roll with an old kitchen knife to get a starter piece of a required length. Use a spade to trim off pieces of sod along a walkway or other hard surface.

Maintenance When the sod is in place, or at least as much as you can lay in a day, soak the sod with water. Don't move the sprinkler until you can lift up a piece of sod and see that the soil beneath it is wet. The edges sometimes roll or curl up because they dry quickly, so make sure they get plenty of water. Continue watering and avoid walking on your new lawn until the sod has firmly established roots in its new soil. How long that will take depends on rainfall and the growing conditions. While a light rain falling on your newly-laid sod each day would be ideal, most likely you'll have to plan on watering on a regular basis to nurture your new lawn.

ANNUALS AND PERENNIALS

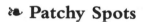 Patchy Spots

Both grass seed and sod can fill in bare spots in lawns. If you have a problem area, such as a shady spot where grass doesn't thrive, consider a specialty grass seed created specifically for that situation. There are many more varieties of grass seed than sod. On the other hand, if a bare spot or area has heavy foot traffic, choose to lay down sod because it will give you instant lawn covering.

If you're seeding over an area with a sparse growth of grass, rake it thoroughly to remove any buildup of thatch and scarify or make light cuts in the soil where the existing grass grows. You need to stir up the soil so the new seed can make contact with it.

PLANTING ANNUALS AND PERENNIALS

*A*nnual flower and vegetable plants go through their life cycle in one year: they live and die in just one growing season. You can start these garden short-sprinters from seed or buy them as seedlings and transplant them. They grow strong and flourish to add instant color and depth in flower beds, around foundation plantings, and in flower boxes and containers.

Perennials are in for the long haul. They are long-term residents of gardens and take more than one year to complete their growing cycle. During winter they rest under a layer of mulch while their roots make new plants that will sprout in the following spring. Many perennials are herbaceous, which means that they die down to the ground when the growing season is over and then reappear next season.

Most plants sold at retail stores have an ID tag attached to them or tucked into the soil. This tag can be confusing because it often gives the Latin or botanical name rather than the common name. For example, one of our favorite ground covers, Bugle, is called *Ajuga reptans*. If you're looking for a certain plant and can't remember its "official" name, use the common name and describe its characteristics. More than likely someone at the nursery can pinpoint it. They'll probably know the Latin name, too.

❧ Layout Guidelines

Here are a few ideas about designing flower beds so they complement other plantings and landscaping materials. In most cases, position tall plants as a backdrop behind lower-growing varieties. A popular design is a three-tier effect, such as having iris or other tall stately flowers along the back of a bed with shorter, bushier plants in front of them and low-growing flowers or border plants as edging material in the very front. A garden bed can be formal with straight-line borders, or more informal and natural looking with curved lines that define it.

Many gardeners use perennials as the backbone of their gardens and fill in with brightly colored annuals like geraniums and petunias. By using both annuals and perennials in your landscaping and garden you'll be guaranteed both lushness and variety throughout the years.

When combined with shrubbery, beds of colorful flowers will soften and add texture to the landscape. Ground cover or any low-growing plant that spreads easily will blend various different plantings together, unifying them very nicely.

If your goal is to add visual interest to a boring green landscape, consider using a bold statement with color. Choose a monochromatic scheme, one that features different types of flowers in variations of one striking color. For example, an array of bright pinks and fuchsias in a corner of a yard can call attention to an otherwise ordinary landscape with an eye-catching affect.

If you like to bring your flowers indoors for flower arrangements or for drying, you might want to have a cutting garden. If that's the case, choose a medley of colorful flowers and tie everything together with a border of white alyssum or unimposing ground cover. For constant color and interest in a garden choose flowers that bloom at various times of the season instead of all at the same time. If the garden space is large, plan room for a stone path or some kind of walkway for easy access to plants.

❧ Preparing the Bed and Planting

The planting technique for both annuals and perennials is the same. Your aim is to secure the plant firmly in the new soil and provide nutrients and water necessary to nurture growth.

If you wish to start your plants from seed see pages 61–66. Here we will deal with how to plant seedlings you buy at a garden center or nursery or those you have started and grown yourself.

If a plant ID tag says it spreads to 3 feet wide, believe it and don't buttonhole it in a tight spot where it has no room to grow. On the other hand, if your goal is to fill a barren area with a bed of flowers, you can get creative about various ways to lay out the plants. When you're replacing annuals from last season or stocking a bed filled with perennials you must work within an already established framework.

Soil preparation   Before you plant anything, prepare the soil and mix in organic matter or fertilizer. Stir up the soil by digging and cultivating it and remove old roots and weeds; then add soil amendments. Use your hands to crumble up small clods of soil.

Before removing the seedlings and plants from their containers position them in the bed so you can get an idea of how everything will look—

sort of a dress rehearsal. Set the containers in the bed and move them around to find the arrangement that suits you best. To help each plant establish itself and stimulate its root system pinch back any growth before transplanting it.

When satisfied, use a hand trowel to dig a hole slightly larger than the root ball of the plant and set the plant in place at the same level as the ground. Make sure the plant is straight and upright and the roots are firmly planted. Move the soil around until it covers the base of the plant.

When planting seedlings from plant cells or flats gently remove each individual seedling from its plastic compartment by squeezing the sides and carefully easing it up and out. This process works best if the soil has been moistened with water first so it will hold together and protect the roots. Poke your finger into the soil and if it is dry and crumbly, give it a sprinkling of water before removing it from its compartment.

To remove a larger plant, such as one in a 6-inch plastic container, make sure that the soil is moist, then turn the container upside down carefully and knock it against the edge of something. The shock will loosen the soil from the inside of the container and the entire plant will come out in one piece. You can also work your hands around the outside of the container, pushing it gently to create a space between it and the soil.

When you remove the plant from its container you'll see how its root system is held together by the soil. Gently poke a finger hole into the soil to loosen it. This will give the plant a little space for it roots to grow. Water the newly planted seedlings and plants after setting them in the ground.

If the plant is in a fibrous container, put the container directly into the ground; it will decompose naturally.

PLANTING BULBS

A bulb is a plant that has the ability to store its food underground. Some of the most popular and easiest to grow bulbs are crocuses, daffodils, tulips, and hyacinths, which herald the end of winter by popping up in early spring. Some bulbs rest underground most of the year. When the soil begins to warm they are ready to send up shoots and bloom. Other bulbs need to be dug up and stored in the fall and then planted in the spring. Digging up those types and planting early-blooming bulbs is often the last gardening act you will perform in the fall. At the same time that you're laying the garden to rest for winter, you're anticipating spring.

You know spring is around the corner at the first sight of daffodil or crocus leaves popping up through the frost-covered soil or a spring snowfall. When they bloom, the tough decision is whether to leave them in the yard as harbingers of spring or to use them as cut flowers indoors to brighten up a room. You can do both by planting a variety of bulbs in more than one place in your yard.

Most people agree that flowering bulbs are most attractive in a natural setting grouped together as a powerful showcase of color instead of planted individually. Use them in clusters with evergreens and foundation plantings and in garden beds as the first plants to bloom. Call attention to a large tree or focal point in a yard by spreading a blanket of flowering bulbs. For a more whimsical look, scatter small bulbs like crocuses throughout the lawn.

For a continual showcase of bulbs, consider planting a selection of bulbs that bloom at various times throughout the spring. For example, snowdrops are usually the first to break through in the spring so they're a good choice. Look for early-flowering varieties of the plants that you like. Talk to someone at a local nursery or garden center who knows the climate and conditions in your area. He or she is the best person to ask for advice about planting bulbs in order to have an ongoing show of springtime flowers.

❧ Laying Down a Blanket of Daffodils

The rule of thumb for planting most bulbs is to plant them three times deeper than their diameter. So a bulb that measures about 2 inches across should be put in a hole about 6 inches deep. The directions on packages of daffodils and many other bulbs tells you to plant them 6 inches deep

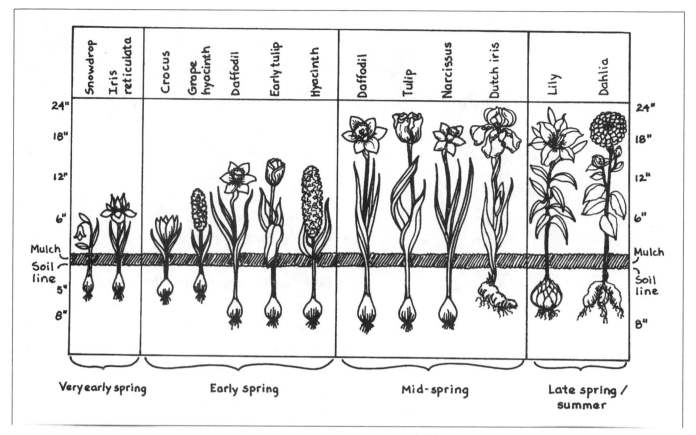

GARDEN BULBS

and 6 to 8 inches apart. Keep in mind that the deeper they're planted, the more they're protected from hungry animals and damage from cold weather.

Choose an area of your yard that has good drainage and preferably plenty of sunshine, although most bulbs will do fine in partial shade.

If you're planting a small number of bulbs, say three or four in a rock garden or in a small area, you may find it easier to plant them individually.

You can buy a bulb planter called a dibble, a kind of cylindrical trowel, that you push into the soil and pull out a plug to create a hole, but your hand trowel will work just as well.

Daffodils and most bulbous plants look their best when they're grouped in cluster, so that's how their bulbs should be planted. Many gardeners feel a cluster of an odd number of bulbs is more attractive than an even number, but that's a matter of choice. The easiest way to plant a lot of

PLANTING SINGLE BULBS

GROUP-PLANTING BULBS

bulbs is to dig up the area with a spade. If your goal is to create a random spread of daffodils in a natural setting but you don't know how to position them, just take a handful of stones and toss them into the air so they fall across the target area. Wherever the stones fall, plant your bulbs.

Whenever you plant bulbs, make sure the soil has been cultivated. If it's an expansive area, use a garden fork; otherwise, break up clumps of soil with a hand trowel so it is granular and easy to work in. Bulbs thrive on bone meal. This natural fertilizer releases its nutrients slowly over a long period of time, so prepare the bed or holes with a sprinkling of it before planting the bulbs.

Position each bulb so that its tip faces upward and it is on even ground so it will grow straight, not at an angle. Gently fill in the soil around the bulbs until the ground is level. Cover planted area with a layer of mulch.

❧ Bulb Maintenance

Bulbs can present a striking appearance in your yard for several years. When they have stopped blooming, remove the dead blossoms so energy goes to their roots. As their leaves dry and turn brown or yellow, don't cut them off. Wait until the leaves come free easily when you pull straight up on them. The leaves are creating food to sustain the bulbs during dormancy so next spring they'll bloom again, often multiplying in number and expanding in size. For some gardeners this untidy mass of dry leaves bothers them so they braid the leaves together before they dry out, makes them look very well-groomed indeed.

After several years, when a bed of daffodils becomes overcrowded or when the flowers are diminishing in size, you can divide them to encourage new and better growth (see pages 89–90).

PLANT A SMALL VEGETABLE PATCH

VEGETABLE GARDEN BOUNTY

*Y*ou can't beat home-grown vegetables for their delicious flavor and mouth-watering appeal which is why more and more of us are becoming one-family farmers. The cost of the seeds, plants, and materials is nothing when compared to the luxury of having fresh produce for the picking in your own backyard. And watching your own vegetable bounty grow and thrive outranks any television show for rewarding viewing.

However, don't let your enthusiasm for planting your first vegetable garden be overcome by unrealistic goals. Temper that energy with common sense and start small, something under 50 square feet. That could be a 6-foot by 8-foot rectangle with a path down the middle, or a row 25 feet long and 2 feet wide. That's still a lot of earth to move and cultivate. All too often an overzealous, inexperienced gardener allocates half

the backyard for vegetables without realizing the care and maintenance it requires.

Location

Location is the most important thing to consider when buying a house. The same is true about choosing a backyard site for planting vegetables. Most vegetables crave sun, so choose a location with at least four and preferably six or more hours of daily sun. Don't get close to trees because their roots take nutrients from the garden. If you can plant your vegetable patch near the kitchen door, so much the better for picking fresh produce from its harvest every day.

Choose an area in the yard where the soil drains naturally and easily. You don't want to

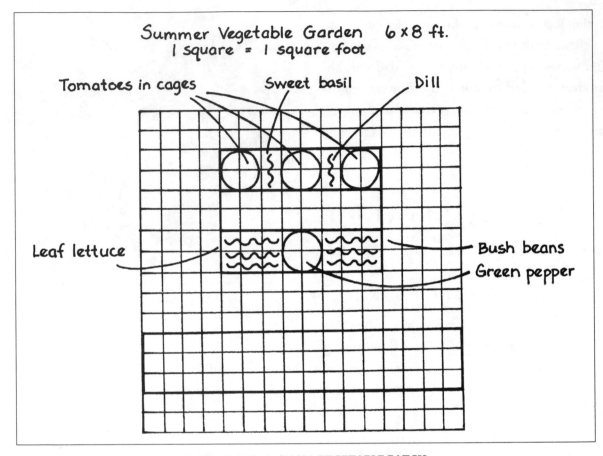

Summer Vegetable Garden 6 × 8 ft.
1 square = 1 square foot

Tomatoes in cages   Sweet basil   Dill

Leaf lettuce

Bush beans
Green pepper

LAYING OUT A SMALL VEGETABLE PATCH

plant vegetables (or anything else for that matter) where rainwater pools and water stagnates. Avoid locating your garden in the direct path of prevailing winds, which can damage stems and branches and uproot plants.

❧ Make a Sketch

Use graph paper to draw a sketch of how you envision your vegetable garden. Make a note of any permanent structures like fencing or a shed.

Then find out how the sun affects the yard—its direction and how many hours it shines on your planned vegetable patch. Make several copies so you try a variety of layouts.

To make your layout meaningful, draw it to scale. Let each square on the graph paper equal either 6 or 12 inches. For example, at 6 inches per square, a 6-foot by 8-foot bed would be 12 squares wide and 16 squares long.

You can configure a vegetable garden in several

ways. Line plants in rows or group them together in clusters. Be sure your plan takes into consideration the spacing that's required between the plants. Since there are literally hundreds of varieties of plants to choose from, each with its own characteristics, be sure to consult the seed packages for specific planting information. You'll find it printed on the back of seed packets or stuck into seedlings container, or listed on a tag. Specific planting information is also included in the plant descriptions in most mail-order gardening catalogs.

If your vegetable garden runs along a physical barrier such as a fence or the wall of a building, plant the tallest crops next to the barrier with shorter plants staggered in size in front of them. Plant tall plants on the north side of the garden so shorter crops aren't in their shade. If you're planting an island-like garden that you can walk all around, place the tallest plants in the middle as a centerpiece and locate shorter and bushier plants in front of them. When possible, take full advantage of the sun by planting vegetables in rows that run east to west.

To make weeding and harvesting easier, incorporate a path or walkway in the plan. You'll be happy you did after your first rainy spell. It's no fun wading in mud to pull weeds or pick tomatoes. Bricks, paving blocks, or crushed stone can be laid down to form a permanent path, or you can use bark chips or some other ground cover or mulch to form the path. See pages 128–131 to learn how to lay a brick garden path.

A good time to plan a new garden is in the fall, before the ground freezes. That will give you time to test the soil in the area you've chosen and to get the soil in shape before the planting season rolls around.

❧ Preparing the Bed

Begin by marking off the area with a string and stakes or by cutting a line around the perimeter with a shovel or spade. Then remove all grass and surface growth and break up the soil. It's hard work digging and shoveling dirt, so take it slow and pace yourself. A garden fork helps in breaking up large clods of soil or turf. Dig the bed 8 to 12 inches deep and then break up the soil so it's loose and pliable. Use a hand cultivator to work the soil and remove pieces of old roots and stones as you move it around. Mix in organic matter and fertilizer and then smooth out and level the soil with a rake.

If you have a large amount of soil to turn over, consider using a rotary tiller, available for rent by the hour or day from your local rental center. Call ahead to reserve one because during the planting season they're in high demand.

❧ Deciding What to Plant

It might seem obvious, but choose only vegetables that your family likes. Sure squash is easy to grow, but if no one in the family likes it, why bother planting it?

There's quite a lot of information about a plant on its label and on the seed packet that can help you decide when and what to grow. The information includes what the plant is, how many days it takes to mature, how many sprouts you can expect, and spacing requirements. Often there are growing tips and a map showing areas of the country keyed to months when it's safe to plant outdoors in warm soil and temperatures.

You can choose between growing vegetables from seed or from starter plants, or by doing a little of both. For your first garden, the National Garden Bureau suggests the following vegetables; all are easy-to-grow from seeds:

Bush green beans
Cucumbers
Leaf lettuces
Garden peas
Pumpkins
Radishes

Summer and
  winter squash
Vegetable spaghetti
  squash
Spinach
Sweet corn

For a large vegetable garden you need plenty

Garden Planting Chart for Vegetables

CROP	DAYS TO MATURITY	NO. OF SEEDS/PLANTS PER 100 SQ. FT.	DISTANCE BETWEEN ROWS	DISTANCE BETWEEN PLANTS	DEPTH TO PLANT
Asparagus	2 seasons	50 roots	3–5 ft.	1$\frac{1}{2}$–2 ft.	6 in.
Beans (bush)	50–60	$\frac{1}{2}$ lb.	3 ft.	2–4 in	1–1$\frac{1}{2}$ in.
Beans (lima)	65–75	1 lb.	2–2$\frac{1}{2}$ ft.	3–4 in.	1–1$\frac{1}{2}$ in.
Beets	55–65	1 oz.	2–2$\frac{1}{2}$ ft. 2 in.	1 in.	$\frac{1}{2}$ in.
Broccoli	60–80	100 plants	2$\frac{1}{2}$ ft.	14–18 in.	$\frac{1}{2}$ in.
Cabbage	65–80	100 plants	2$\frac{1}{2}$ ft.	12 in.	1 in.
Cantaloupe	80–90	1 oz.	4–6 ft.	3$\frac{1}{2}$–4 ft.	1$\frac{1}{2}$ in.
Carrots	70–80	$\frac{1}{2}$ oz.	2 ft.	2–3 in.	$\frac{1}{2}$ in.
Cauliflower	55–60	100 plants	3 ft.	12–18 in.	$\frac{1}{2}$ in.
Corn	80–100	$\frac{1}{4}$ lb.	3–3$\frac{1}{2}$ ft.	12–18 in.	2 in.
Cucumbers	60–65	1 oz.	4$\frac{1}{2}$–5 ft.	3–4 ft.	1$\frac{1}{2}$ in.
Eggplant	75–90	50 plants	3 ft.	10 in.	$\frac{1}{2}$ in.

Garden Planting Chart for Vegetables

CROP	DAYS TO MATURITY	NO. OF SEEDS/PLANTS PER 100 SQ. FT.	DISTANCE BETWEEN ROWS	DISTANCE BETWEEN PLANTS	DEPTH TO PLANT
Lettuce	60–85	1/2 oz.	2–2 1/2 ft.	10–12 in.	1/2 in.
Okra	55–60	1 oz.	3–3 1/2 ft.	6 in.	1 in.
Onions	100–120	300 plants	1–2 ft.	3–4 in.	3/4 in.
Peas (garden)	60–80	1 lb.	2 1/2 ft.	1 in.	1 1/2–2 in.
Peppers	65–80	50 plants	2 1/2 ft.	1 1/2–2 ft.	1/4 in.
Potatoes (white)	70–90	1 peck	2 1/2–3 ft.	10–14 in.	5 in.
Potatoes (sweet)	90–150	100 plants	3 1/2 ft.	12 in.	6 in.
Radishes	25–30	1 oz.	1 1/2 ft.	1 in.	1/2 in.
Spinach	40–45	1 oz.	1 1/2–2 ft.	1–2 in.	3/4 in.
Squash (summer)	40–60	1 oz.	3–5 ft.	2 ft.	1 1/2 in.
Squash (winter)	85–90	1/2 oz.	5 ft.	3 ft.	1 1/2–2 in.
Tomatoes	70–85	50 plants	3–4 ft.	2 1/2–3 ft.	1/2 in.
Turnips	45–65	1/2 oz.	1–2 ft.	1 2 in.	1/2 in.
Watermelon	80–90	1 oz.	10 ft.	8–10 ft.	1 1/2 in.

of space. The accompanying table lists the most popular vegetables with their space and planting requirements and how long it takes to grow them.

❧ Planting Seeds

You can use the same procedure for sowing seeds in the garden as for sowing them indoors (see pages 61–66). But keep in mind that the outdoor environment is more hostile so your success rate may not be as high. Make sure the soil is rich with organic matter and finely graded. Water the bed gently before sowing the seeds. Plant the seeds in furrows or rows, but don't press down too firmly. Some gardeners like to spread a thin layer of mulch over seedlings to prevent them from being washed away in rain or a heavy sprinkling. To save space you can sow seeds more closely than the suggested spacing and when seedlings have germinated you can thin them to the proper distance. It's important that the tiny seeds don't get drowned or washed away before they have a chance to germinate. Water them gently every day if there's no rain. Most vegetable seeds will germinate in seven to fourteen days if the soil temperature and moisture are adequate. The new sprouts will need thinning, so remove the weakest of the young seedlings to provide growing room for the stronger ones.

Weeds will creep into the bed, but don't be overzealous unless you're positive you're plucking out a pest and not a young sprout. As the sprouts grow and spread you may have to reposition them. Do this carefully and gently, disturbing their roots as little as possible.

❧ Planting Starter Plants or Seedlings

For best results, the first-time gardener should purchase starter plants or seedlings to grow the following vegetables.

Cabbage	**Onions**
Cantaloupe	**Peppers**
Eggplant	**Tomatoes**
Okra	**Watermelon**

By following the spacing requirements or growing room listed in the planting table you can put seedlings in place and not have to disturb them. Use the individual plants in their containers to get an idea of spacing. Position them on the soil as you work out your scheme, allowing enough room to weed around them and reach their fruit.

Envisioning just how large a tomato seedling will grow can be difficult, and you'll probably think it looks downright silly to see tiny seedlings set so far apart from each other. But as the growing season sets in and the plants begin to flourish you'll be glad you paid attention to their spacing requirements.

Plant the seedlings in the soil at the depth suggested in the table. Be sure the hole has been moistened with water and amended with organic matter. As you fill in the soil around a seedling,

PLANTING VEGETABLE SEEDLINGS

take care in your positioning it. Set it in the soil at the same height it was in its container and spread a light topping of soil over it. If you are planting peat pots or biodegradable containers set them directly in the ground. Cut off the top rim of the container so it doesn't stick up but is concealed under the ground, where it will naturally decompose.

Spread a layer of mulch around the plants to help retain moisture and prevent weeds from invading. When weeds pop out, as surely they will, use a hand cultivator or a rake with short stiff prongs to scratch around the soil. Disturb the surface layer and you'll be able to pull out the weed with ease. Throughout the growing cycle, watch for signs of stress and keep the vegetables watered and free of pests.

MULCH BETWEEN PLANTS

PLANT GROUND COVER

Ground cover is low-growing, ground-hugging perennial plants that carpet an area with blossoms or, more often, richly colored foliage. Many varieties of plants make excellent ground covers. You should choose a single type for a given area, some variety that requires little or no maintenance. Grass is a ground cover, but

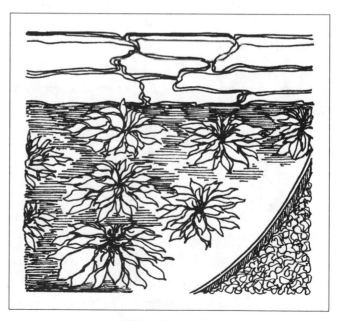

GROUND COVER

it is not particularly decorative and it requires constant maintenance.

❧ Choosing Ground Cover

To blanket the base of a tree choose shallow-rooted ground covers such as periwinkle, woodruff, or violets that won't compete with the tree roots for nutrients in the soil. You can also plant ajuga and ivy to spread over tree roots and to fill in lonely bare spots under evergreens and shrubs. An edible ground cover like strawberry plants will grow nicely in a sunny spot, perhaps alongside a walkway from house to garden. In addition to their appearance, strawberries offer a bonus of fruit that you can eat fresh or make into preserves. The plants will produce fruit for years to come. Pachysandra is another popular border plant often used along walkways and around hard-surface areas such as patios and driveways.

Once they are established, ground covers are usually maintenance free. They act like mulch in preserving moisture and choking out weeds so other plants can thrive. Ground covers are particularly well suited for sloped areas that are difficult to reach and maintain. Once rooted they spread, often with abandon, until they blanket an area. Of course, if left unchecked ground cover can become a nuisance. Because of its persistence and tenacity ground cover can virtually take over a garden and become a number one pest.

To control ground cover from encroaching be-

yond its limits enclose it in an edging. Use brick, paving stones, rubber strips, or landscape lumber to holds its growth in check (see Edging a Garden Bed, pages 88–89). Other ways to keep it in control is to cut it back, and to find friends who want to transplant it to their yards.

The rate at which a ground cover spreads is an important detail to consider when choosing what kind to plant. For example, pachysandra is a lovely ground cover but it takes much longer to get established than ajuga or ivy. Also consider the conditions in the area you want to cover. There are many varieties of ground cover well suited for difficult growing conditions. For example lily of the valley, violets, or liriope grow well in shady areas; ajuga grows well in soil that is too dry for many other varieties.

Before you go out and buy any plants, ask your friends if they have any ground cover they'd like to get rid of. If you do the work of digging up the plants, many people will gladly share them with you. You need only enough to put a plant every 2 feet or so; they will spread to cover the area in a season or two.

Some ground covers have deep root systems, others have a shallow runner system that spreads throughout the soil. When digging up ground cover to transplant to your garden, use a trowel and remove as much soil surrounding the roots as possible. Spread the plants loosely and lay them in an open box or container to transport them to your yard. Get them in the ground right away, planting them at the same depth at which they were growing.

If you can't find a source of free ground cover, talk to the folks at your local nursery and garden center. They can recommend the best growing and spreading varieties for your particular area.

❧ Coverage

Measure the area where you plan to use ground cover before shopping so you know how much you want covered. Information about how far and how fast a ground cover spreads is printed on the plant label. In most cases the number of plants you buy will depend on your budget, or how long you are willing to wait for the plants to spread naturally and blanket the area.

For example, the label for ajuga suggests that you space plants 12 to 15 inches apart. If you have an area that's $1^1/2$ by 5 feet to cover, you could purchase five plants and place them 12 inches apart along the centerline of the length. In a couple of years they will spread to cover the entire area. Or you could purchase ten plants and place them closer together, filling in the area in a random pattern. By the end of a growing season the area should begin to be nicely covered.

❧ Planting

Prepare the soil as you would for planting any other type of plant by cultivating it and mixing in some compost or nutrients (see pages 13–17). Most ground covers can be planted about 6 inches deep, but check the specific requirements for your plants. Ground covers are sold in individual containers, in large flats, or in bundles of roots and cuttings. Handle the individual plants gently; separate bundled plants carefully before putting them into the prepared soil. Cover the ground all around the plants with a light mulch to fight weed growth and retain moisture. Mulch does a nice job of covering up the bare spots between ground cover plants while they spread and grow.

PLANT A WILDFLOWER MAT

If you would like an area to produce a profusion of blooms such as wildflowers, you can plant seeds by hand, or you can save a great deal of work by using a seed fabric. A seed fabric is a mat of hay and biodegradable mulching material impregnated with seed and fertilizer. It looks like a straw blanket rolled out in a garden until the seeds germinate and the hay and mulch decompose. The mat retains moisture while holding the seeds and soil in place, and the supplemental plant nutrients help the seeds to germinate and take root. The seeds are held to the bottom of the mat with a water-soluble adhesive;

A WILDFLOWER MAT CAN FILL A LARGE AREA WITH BLOOMS

has a minimum of six hours of direct sunlight a day. For best results plant the mat when the soil is a warm 70° to 72°F.

Preparing the Soil

Use a garden fork and rake to loosen clumps of soil and remove any stones, roots, and weeds. Cultivate the soil so that it is crumbly and coarse to at least a depth of 1/2 inch. Grade the soil with a rake so that it is level and water it just before you lay down the wildflower mat.

Laying Down the Seed Fabric

Unroll the mat next to the prepared bed with the

as the glue emulsifies with watering, the seeds drop into the soil.

You'll find seed mats sold in several mail-order gardening catalogs as well as in large garden centers. The mats come in 12- and 18-inch-wide rolls from 5 to 15 feet long. They contain seeds that will produce flowers that bloom at different times, so you'll have an ongoing cascade of flowers throughout the season. This all-in-one approach to gardening is available with seeds for wildflowers, flowering annuals, or vegetables.

Location

Choose an area for your wildflower garden that

LAY THE MAT OVER DAMP SOIL

bottom (seed) side facing down, toward the soil. To make sure, look for the sticker that says "This side DOWN." If you have to cut it to fit the area, use a pair of household scissors or a utility knife. Then roll up the mat so you can position it on the damp soil.

Unroll the blanket and make certain that the seed side is in contact with the soil. If the fabric corners won't lie flat, secure them with some stones so they don't curl up. Sprinkle the mat with at least 1/2 inch of water to ensure that the blanket is touching the soil and to release the seeds into the soil.

Keep the mat damp to provide a germination environment. While it will take a good six weeks before you see wildflowers in bloom you should see seedlings in seven to fourteen days. If any seedlings are too close to each other, relocate them very carefully.

These flower mats are relatively new, so don't be surprised at a few questioning glances from traditional gardeners. What starts out looking like a straw rug will eventually becomes a lovely showcase of colorful blooms you'll enjoy all season.

PLANT A KID'S GARDEN

Working with a child in the garden is enjoyable and rewarding because the two of you can share the wonders of nature watching plants grow. Gardening time can be a meaningful time that is both productive and reflective. In addition, it's fun to muck about in the soil and witness a live show of blooming flowers and mouth-watering vegetables.

Children like to have their own space—their own room in the house. Give them personal space in a sunny spot in the garden too. If your yard is small and heavily shaded, make it a container garden that you can move to the best growing conditions. Use a window box or some clay pots, whatever you have that can con-

CHILDREN WILL TAKE PRIDE IN
GARDENS OF THEIR OWN

tain soil in a sunny spot.

Think small, not big, so your child's first gardening experience is more fun than work. You want him or her coming back for more, without dreading the weeding chores.

Remember that a child has a short attention span, so plan to do a variety of tasks, and not just a single activity. Kids like to move and mess around in the soil so make sure they dress in "anything goes" clothing. If your child is squeamish about worms and other crawly creatures, provide a pair of old gloves (not mittens).

Be patient and relaxed with a beginner. You might shudder at the sight of an uneven row of plants but your young gardener probably isn't so fussy. You want to nurture the love of gardening in this first experience, so bite your tongue when your child's efforts don't meet your standards. You can always foster better work habits next season, but only if the child is hooked on gardening the first time.

Show that you are proud of your youngster's garden by putting up a small sign on a stake identifying the patch as "Amy's Garden," "Tomatoes by Jake," or something similar.

❧ Choosing Plants for a Kid's Garden

The best advice about what to plant in a child's garden comes from the National Garden Bureau, which suggests a combination of easy-to-grow vegetables and flowers. Carrots, radishes, and to-matoes are good vegetable choices. If you have room for vines, consider mini-pumpkins.

For flowers the Garden Bureau suggests varieties that can be used as cut flowers or decorations, such as zinnias, marigolds, snapdragons and forget-me-nots. Plant a few sunflower seeds if you want to see something really spectacular. They'll grow from 2 to 10 feet tall.

Other interesting plants for a kid's garden include the following, from the National Garden Bureau's list "Some Fun Plants to Grow":

Calceolaria. Called the "pocketbook" plant, the blooms resemble old-fashioned purses.

Four O'Clocks. Easy to grow from seed, these colorful flowers don't open until mid to late afternoon. Hence the name.

Torenia. The "wishbone plant." Inside the blooms is a small ridge shaped just like a wishbone.

Lunaria. The "money plant" forms disc-shaped seed pods that can be rubbed and polished to resemble a silvery quarter-sized coin.

Scallop squash. Summer squash that resembles a flying saucer.

Impatiens. "Blizzy Lizzy" or "impatient" plant. The ripe seed pods burst open to scatter seed. Put a fat one in your hand and press lightly for a good tickle when it bursts.

Sweet peas. Dwarf or climbing, these lovely flowers have the same name as the character in Popeye cartoons. Maybe you should plant them next to the spinach.

🌱 Getting Started

A trowel and short-handled weeder can be grasped comfortably by a child's small hand but most long-handled tools, like shovels or full-size rakes can be too long and cumbersome. In most garden centers you'll find downsized garden tools suitable for a child. They're designed for hand size and stature. Children can also use toy beach or sandbox shovels, or old kitchen utensils like a large baking spoon or spatula.

Help the child cultivate the soil together so preparing the bed goes quickly. Pick a day when the soil is crumbly, not too dry or wet. Use a hand trowel and cultivator to work the soil back and forth and squash the lumps so they disappear. To encourage involvement don't lecture, let the child ask questions. Be informative in your answers. For example, explain that adding organic matter makes the soil richer and adds nutrients so plants can grow strong and healthy. Explain what nutrients are.

A combination of sowing seeds and planting seedlings is a nice way to introduce gardening to a youngster, because he or she will witness new growth from seeds and watch faster-growing seedlings take off. To sow seeds, let the child create a furrow in the soil and sprinkle the seeds in rows. To help small hands with this delicate job put the seeds in a spoon for sprinkling.

When you're planting seedlings in holes refer to the plant labels for some guidelines about spacing and placement. Let the child dig the hole and position the seedlings, smooth the soil, and then spread mulch around the new plants.

Don't forget to water. While you're at it, talk about keeping the new seeds and seedlings moist while their roots are making claims in the soil around them. Let the child use a watering can or hose to water the patch.

🌱 Maintaining a Garden

Children seem to enjoy the chore of maintaining a garden as much as planting one, so take advantage of that enthusiasm. Encourage them to pull pesky weeds that poke through the soil; show how to pull a weed straight out of the ground, not at an angle, to get all of its roots. Caution them about pulling out new seed sprouts by mistake.

🌱 Harvesting

A toddler with a fistful of flower blooms proudly pinched from a garden bed may look cute, but that's not the kind of harvesting to promote. If a child can't operate a pair of garden shears then he or she is probably too small to cut a stemmed flower. That's where your help is needed.

Vegetables are another matter because they are picked by hand. As you see the tomatoes ripen and the carrot tops sprout out of the ground, use the opportunity to show and tell your young gardener how to carefully pick them from the stem or pull them out of the ground. After a little practice kids can do it themselves.

EDGING A GARDEN BED

$\mathcal{E}$dging defines the borders of a lawn, garden bed, or other planted area. The least expensive edging requires only your labor. You use a spade or edging tool to dig a narrow, shallow

CUTTING AN EDGING TRENCH OR SLIT

trench that outlines a garden bed. This mini-ditch keeps grass and weeds from encroaching into the bed. It also helps keep the lawnmower out of the flower bed. For the best-looking results lay out a guideline for the edging before you begin and maintain a constant depth all along the trench. Every year you'll have to redig it to maintain a sharp, crisp edging.

You'll find a host of edging materials sold in garden centers and home centers designed to trim out your garden. You can buy edging made of wood, brick of various shapes and sizes, and rubber or plastic strips. This is more costly, but often more effective and attractive than a simple trench.

Pressure-treated 2 × 4 lumber can be used for straight stretches of a flower garden. Because the preservatives used in such wood may be toxic, and even approved nontoxic preservatives are dangerous to some individuals, take these precautions when working with pressure-treated material. Wear gloves; don't handle the wood with your bare hands; and wear a long-sleeve shirt when sawing or drilling the wood. Also wear eye, nose, and mouth protection. Do not burn any scrap wood or sawdust.

To lay an edging of bricks dig a trench and fill it with a shallow base of sand. You can lay bricks lengthwise flat on the ground or end-to-end on their sides. Or you can set them on their ends, straight up or at an angle for a decorative effect.

Rubber and plastic strips are easy to cut and

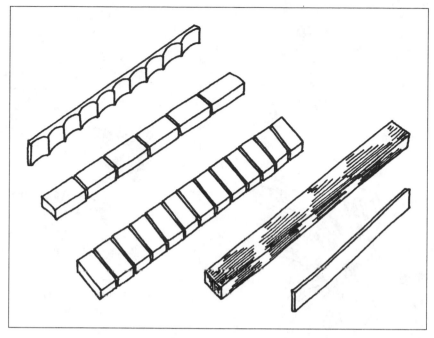

TYPES OF EDGING MATERIALS

bend around curves. You'll find modular edging blocks of wood or brick that are small and easy to install in various configurations.

Set the edging materials at the same height or just above the level of the plant bed. If the ground is uneven, adjust the height as you work your way around the garden.

DIVIDING PLANTS

Flowers such as daylilies, peonies, lilies of the valley, and other multistemmed peren-

nials are a bonus because they can be divided to propagate new plants. Such plants grow new shoots above the ground at their crown. As they grow over the years the center section of the plant is crowded out and often dies or rots, leaving a ring of new plants.

You can separate this new growth into individual plants with roots, stem, and foliage to transplant elsewhere. Ground covers and bulbs are other good candidates for plant division. You can get several plants by dividing one large mature plant.

Plan on dividing a plant during the coolest part of the day, preferably when the sun isn't

USE TWO FORKS TO DIVIDE A LARGE PLANT INTO SMALLER SECTIONS

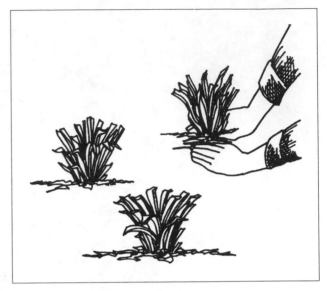

SPACE DIVIDED SECTIONS TO ALLOW FOR FUTURE SPREADING

shining to avoid stressing the plant due to loss of moisture and being uprooted. If you're transplanting in the fall, trim off the top of the foliage; if you're making the division in the spring, leave the foliage intact.

Before dividing a plant make holes for the new plants so you can transplant the divided parts right away. Then water the plant thoroughly to soften the soil and make dividing easier.

Use a shovel, spade, or garden fork to dig into the center of the plant and force it into two parts. You'll be amazed at how tough and resistant the roots are. In some cases it helps to separate the roots using two garden tools when dividing plants. To do that dig down with both tools and apply force to one, and then the other. In a large plant there are actually several individual plants that you can cut apart. Relocate each divided plant with its own root system to its new spot in the garden, making sure it is planted at the same depth as before.

Tend the transplants carefully with plenty of water, and protect them with mulch.

PLANT AN ORNAMENTAL VINE

FLOWERING VINES CAN BEAUTIFY AND CONCEAL

Given enough time and encouragement, a vine can grow up a wall or tree, down a slope, or completely camouflage a fence. A colorful morning glory weaving a path along a wire fence or a clematis winding its way around a gate post can add a soft natural flow of color in any yard. Vines can disguise an imperfect foundation or cover an open fence with foliage so it's an attractive visual barrier.

Vines can also be very aggressive plants that need no encouragement to grow. Some, like honeysuckle and ivy, are so vigorous that they may threaten to take over your garden and cover every fence or tree in the yard.

Vines attach themselves in various ways. Some twine or wind their stems around a support, others send out tendrils that look like thin strands of thread. These strands wrap around whatever they touch. Still other vines attach themselves using little projections called holdfasts that act like small suction cups and stick to most objects that they contact. Vines aren't very particular what they climb. It can be fencing, the siding of your house, or the bark or branches of a tree.

When choosing a vine for its decorative or masking properties, consider how much sunlight and shade it will receive. Some vines need a great deal of sun, others do not. Know the size of the area you want the vine to cover so you can decide how many plants are needed.

◆ Planting

Plant an ornamental vine by studying the direction of its spreading vines or branches and then position it accordingly. If the offshoot of the plant is short, it won't be as noticeable as a longer one that tends to lean in a particular direction. Dig a hole with a trowel deep enough for the roots to have plenty of room to grow. Cultivate

SUPPORT VINES WITH SOFT, LOOSE TIES

unwanted shoots and any that get too long and leggy. Don't let the vine get overgrown, otherwise parts will die, and dead wood restrains a plant's growth.

To trim an extremely overgrown vine selectively, cut down some of its branches to the ground, leaving others to begin anew. Choose a few of the best shoots and train them as a new vine. Remove all the dead wood and thin out the toughest stems to the ground so air can circulate around the plant and water can get to its roots.

the soil and add organic matter or compost. Position the plant so it can spread and grow without interference and then cover the roots with soil. Secure the offshoots or branches with soft string, shoelaces, or paper-wrapped twist wires. Position and secure them loosely, without kinking, so the vine has plenty of spreading room.

🍃 Vine Maintenance

During the first season, lightly prune any broken stems or branches. Over winter, protect the vine's root system with a covering of mulch. Then in early spring add organic matter to the soil around the plant, prune the vine to shape, and remove dead branches or stems. Remove any

PLANT A FLOWERING SHRUB

*T*he beautiful blossoms of flowering shrubs can be an important ingredient in home landscaping. Their color and texture make them attractive as a focal point in a yard or as one of the elements of a landscape design. Planting shrubs is relatively easy; choosing what kind to plant is more challenging because of the great variety available. Flowering shrubs usually require little or no maintenance, but they will give you years of enjoyment.

A shrub is a woody plant that usually has several stems and is smaller than a tree; most shrubs are well under 15 feet tall. Some are evergreens, others are deciduous and lose their leaves at some point in their yearly cycle.

Because of their variety, you can find a shrub suitable for any spot in your landscaping. Older homes in established areas are likely to have a lovely lilac bush planted in a backyard corner or a row of sprawling bridal wreath alongside the house. Large flowering shrubs are used to anchor a landscape; low-growing shrubs often spread over a rock garden or border a fence. They are best left in a natural shape and can be used alone or in a row as hedging material. Azaleas, rhododendrons, and lilacs are popular choices, but the list seems endless when it comes to making a choice.

For information about which flowering shrubs will thrive in your area, consult a local garden center or nursery. The inventory will vary during the year and the selection may not be large toward the end of the summer, but most of the time you can find a dazzling assortment of flowering shrubs in stock or quickly available on order.

Most small shrubs are sold in containers in which they are grown. Indicators of a good healthy shrub are a vibrant leaf color and a well-balanced shape. Avoid plants that are lopsided or shapeless. The shrub should also look comfortably fitted in the container, without roots bulging at the top or spilling over the rim.

DECORATIVE SHRUBS OFFER GREAT VARIETY

❧ Planting

To plant a shrub, first spend time preparing the hole carefully. It must be a welcoming new environment. Dig the hole at least twice as wide as the container and one and a half times as deep. Use a spade to dig the hole and a garden fork to break up the soil that you remove.

Water the shrub in its container so the soil is moist. Tap the sides of the container to loosen the soil and gently tilt the container to one side as you ease the plant and soil out of it, next to the hole. If it doesn't come out easily, cut away the container with a utility knife.

Position the shrub firmly on the level bottom

**PLANT THE ROOT BALL FLUSH WITH THE
SURROUNDING SOIL**

at a later date to correct its position can cause harm.

Remove any tags or wires wrapped around the branches. If any branches snapped during the planting process, use pruning shears to trim them off. Also remove any stray or crossover branches that will obstruct the growth of the plant. Don't forget to water it weekly.

PLANT A HEDGE

of the hole and hold it straight as you fill in soil around it. Mix in some organic matter or compost with the soil and occasionally add water to prevent air pockets from forming beneath the soil. Work the soil around and spread it in a mound at the base of the shrub. The soil should be at the same level as it was in the container. Look at the bark of the plant and you'll notice a darkened ring around it. Don't pile the soil any higher around the plant than this marking or you risk smothering the shrub.

Stand back and look at the plant to make sure that it is straight and in the correct position. Now is the time to straighten it if necessary. Soon the roots will begin to spread and establish themselves outside the original root ball. Digging up a shrub

A hedge is a living fence that provides a dense green backdrop or barrier on your property. It can create privacy by enclosing a yard

**HEDGES ARE AN ATTRACTIVE WAY TO MARK
BOUNDARIES AND OBTAIN PRIVACY**

and it will help block noise and wind. Evergreens and holly are popular choices for hedging material, but throughout the country nurseries carry shrubs they strongly recommend for endurance and hardiness in local conditions.

While the most common hedge is a straight row of shrubs, you can plant a natural hedge in a curved or winding informal row, or in a line that follows the contour of a landscape. Before you start digging and planting, make sure that you know the boundaries of your property. You'll find your property line on the plot survey of your house. Most banks and loan institutions require a plot survey when a house changes owners. So study the survey and check the limits of your property. Anything over the line becomes your neighbor's or may have to be moved if it encroaches on public or private property.

🐚 Planting

You can plant a hedge by digging individual holes for the plants or by digging a trench the entire length of the row. Use a string and stakes to establish a straight row. Lay down rope or garden hose or pour a thin line of sand to mark a curved or winding row.

If you are planting a row of privet it is probably easiest to dig a trench because the plants should be placed close together. You can adjust the placement of the shrubs before filling in soil around them. For a tight, dense hedge stagger the plants in two rows.

Larger hedge plants such as evergreens, which spread as they grow, should be spaced farther apart and are probably better planted in separate holes. Space the shrubs along the layout string or line and use the base of each plant as a guide for digging its hole.

Whatever method you choose, make sure the shrubs will have plenty of growing room. Follow the spacing requirements specified on the plant ID tag.

As you position each plant make sure it is sitting upright and has plenty of fertilizer or organic matter added to the soil. Build up the soil around the hedge so it is at the same level as in the plant container (see pages 119–121). Be sure to remove

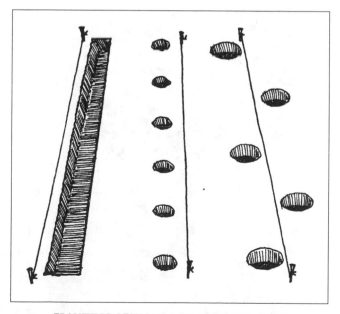

PLANTING OPTIONS FOR HEDGE PLANTS

any tags or wires from the branches so they don't restrict growth after planting.

❧ Caring for a Hedge

Hedges can be formal or informal, depending on how you prune and shape them. After planting a hedge, use pruning shears to remove any broken or dead branches. For an informal hedge, prune the plants to follow their natural contour, just as when pruning an individual plant. Let the shrubs be themselves. Trim them so the branches don't restrict each other, and remove dried or dead shoots at the base of the plant. There will be open spaces or gaps between some of the plants, so at first the hedge will not provide a complete barrier, but it will fill in with growth.

TREES ADD BEAUTY AND VALUE TO A PROPERTY

To prune a more formal hedge that will become a dense thick wall of foliage you must do some shaping. Above all, avoid a top-heavy hedge, one in which the top is wider than the bottom. A top-heavy shape blocks the sun out and reduces air circulation, which can stifle the growth of the lower branches. Prune the hedge so the sides are vertical, or angle them a bit so top is narrower than the bottom. As time goes by the base of the plant will fill out, creating a lush green living fence.

PLANT A TREE

You won't forget the day you plant a tree in your yard because it's like bringing home a guest who stays forever. As the tree blossoms and grows, you'll often reflect on its small and spindly beginnings. You'll feel the pain when its branches break in a lightning storm and nurture it back to life with loving care.

A tree melds into the landscape as if it had always been there. As the tree matures, so may your family grow from tiny tots who play in its protective shadow to industrious kids who built a house in its branches.

To help you decide the type and size of tree to plant, make a sketch of your yard. Perhaps you already have a suitable sketch made for other projects. It can be rough but it should include an outline of the house and any other buildings, notes about existing trees and landscaping, and the location of any driveways or walkways. If you're planning to build a deck or erect a swing set someday, mark down the position. The sketch should be drawn to scale and include distances between buildings and trees and anything that might affect where you plant a tree.

You will probably have a good idea where you want to plant a tree before getting started on the project. Locate the area on your plan and check to see if it provides ample room for the tree to spread and grow. For a new tree to prosper it should not be placed under the shadow of another tree. Don't locate a tree too close to your house nor at the very edge of your lot. Refer to the plot survey of your house to be sure you are planting the tree on your property, not on your neighbor's or on public property.

Look overhead to see if there are utility lines running across the area. You don't want to plant directly under overhead cables and have the utility company cut off the top of your tree when it grows too high. Avoid future problems by planting a tree in an area where it can spread and grow unobstructed.

In order to plant even a small tree you must dig a sizable hole, so make certain that there are no underground cables or pipes where you want to plant your tree. Call your local Miss Utility Center or your local utility companies. Miss Utility Centers are supported by regional utility companies to promote their "call before you dig" programs. You supply your name and address and the center passes that information to their member utility companies in your area. The utility companies will send someone to mark any underground utility lines in your yard. The markers are color coded to identify each line. If you have a septic tank, you must not plant over the line from the house to the tank, over the tank, or close to the pipes in the leach field. Tree roots can clog a septic system quickly.

Choosing a Tree

Know what you want the tree to do before considering its cost and size. Do you want the tree to shade your house in the summer months or to act as a windbreak across a vacant lot? Do you need instant shade or can you wait a few years for the tree to grow? The cost of a tree is determined by several factors, but size and species characteristics are most significant. The smaller and the more ordinary the tree, the cheaper it will be.

Some trees are deciduous, which means they drop their leaves in the cold season. Oaks and elms are examples of this type. Deciduous species make good shade trees in the summer; in winter their bare branches allow the sunlight to shine through, providing potential solar heating. However, without leaves deciduous trees do not make good winter windbreaks.

**BE SURE THE TREE IS FIRMLY SEATED AND UPRIGHT
BEFORE FILLING THE PLANTING HOLE**

**SURROUND A NEWLY-PLANTED TREE WITH A MOUND
OF SOIL AND MULCH**

Trees that don't lose their foliage but stay green all year are called evergreens. Fir and pine are examples of this type. They can provide shade but are best as windbreaks since they hold their foliage throughout the year. Evergreens are usually fast growers.

If you are a new homeowner faced with an empty backyard, your budget may determine how many and what size of trees you can purchase. If that's the case, work out a long-term overall landscape plan for your property with the help of a nursery or a landscape planner. Then you can add trees and materials over a period of time as your budget allows.

❧ Safe Transport for a Tree

If you have or can rent a pickup truck or a van, you can save money by taking your tree home; but don't invest in a tree and then damage it in transport. It may be better to pay to have the tree delivered, especially if it needs two or more people to handle it.

If you do move it yourself, lay the root ball gently on the truck or van bed. Then move it all the way to the front of the truck so it will not slide around if you have to brake quickly. In an open truck, cover the tree with an old blanket to shield it from wind; tie or pin the blanket so it can't blow off. Wind pulls moisture out of the tree, especially if it has leaves. A fifteen-minute ride in an open truck on a hot dry summer day can severely damage an uncovered young tree.

Remember that driving 30 or 40 miles an hour can create air currents that have hurricane force as far as a tree is concerned.

❧ Digging the Hole

The roots of trees grow more horizontally than vertically, so dig a hole that's at least twice as wide as the root ball and at least one and a half times as deep. The soil line of the tree should be the same as its line at the nursery. As you dig the hole, break up the soil so it is loose and crumbly and pile it to one side. Then mix in organic matter. Set the tree in the center of the hole. Make sure it is on a sound footing and standing up straight. Fill in around the root ball with the soil, occasionally sprinkling in water to prevent air pockets from forming.

The soil should form a gentle mound with the tree growing out of the center. Use a grading rake to smooth the soil and spread a 2- to 4-inch layer of mulch over the mound. It also helps to create a catch basin to retain as much rain water as possible so it can soak into the ground around the young tree. Pile up excess soil around the circumference of the hole to form a low dike.

An overzealous lawn cutter can damage a newly planted tree by banging into it with the mower. To protect the tree trunk from such damage consider using a barrier wrap. One version is made of brown plastic that expands as the tree grows. It has holes in it so the tree can breathe and air can circulate around it. Apply the wrap to the base of the tree trunk, winding it around to protect the lower portion of the trunk. Also, add padded guy wires or ropes to provide support against wind for at least the first year; see pages 44–45.

Finally, be sure to protect your investment in your tree by watering the new tree often during hot spells or if there is not enough rain.

FOUNDATION PLANTINGS

Shrubs or a border of plants along the foundation of a house will frame visually and often will conceal unattractive building material such as concrete blocks. In addition to hiding the foundation, plantings can add color and texture to the surroundings. Yews, junipers, and various evergreens are popular choices because of their longevity and enduring qualities.

Foundation plantings can also correct an architectural weakness or call attention to an attractive feature. For example, a house set high with too much foundation exposed can be lowered visually with shrubs planted at the corners to give the illusion of width. A grouping of low shrubbery with higher plantings on either side can frame a bay window.

In new homes where the foundation of a house is often wrapped in vinyl siding to match

**FOUNDATION PLANTINGS MAKE A GRACEFUL
TRANSITION BETWEEN HOUSE AND GARDEN
OR YARD LANDSCAPING**

from rainfall, especially if your garden hose can't reach it.

A common mistake is setting shrubs too close to the house. As they grow (as they surely will), the branches push against the house, often breaking off and damaging the plants. Planning ahead makes all the difference.

❧ Planning the Site

It may seem awkward to plant a small shrub 2 or 3 feet from a house but if the mature size is 36 inches in diameter, then it will need ample growing space all around. As you look at nursery stock the house there's nothing to hide. But the line where the house meets the soil often needs softening and color. Because a house has straight lines and sharp corners consider planting shrubbery at the foundation that varies in height. A pleasing effect features high plantings in the rear and lower ones in the front. To break the shades of green in a grouping, include a flowering shrub, or place a group of them at a corner.

The size and color of shrubbery is important when choosing foundation plantings, but so is a plant's watering requirements. Don't choose a water-hungry shrub for an area that is sheltered

**SPACE PLANTS TO ALLOW FOR SPREADING
AS THEY GROW**

and shrubs, check the ID tags about the mature spread in inches or feet.

Follow the same guidelines as for planting any new shrubbery (see pages 92–94). Since you may be working in a tight corner or between existing shrubs, you may have to use a trowel instead of a shovel. Be as resourceful as you can under the conditions.

Use ground covers (see pages 81–83) among foundation plantings to choke out weed growth, and plant brightly colored annuals to add interest.

PLANT A LIVE CHRISTMAS TREE

For a long time people who lived in the country with land to spare have been using live Christmas trees for the holidays and then planting them on their property. Recently, many suburban dwellers have followed suit. If you have talked to anyone who has decorated a tree and then planted it in the yard, you can see the pleasure it brings. The tree is a benchmark of time and always a source of enjoyment as it grows to new heights with every passing Christmas. It's also a nice alternative to using the same old artificial tree or discarding an expensive cut tree year after year.

Local nurseries and garden centers sell living Christmas trees potted in containers or with the root ball wrapped in burlap. The selections offered are suitable for growing in the local area; they are survivors that can thrive where you live. Spruce, fir, and pines are just a few examples.

A LIVING CHRISTMAS TREE IS A GIFT WITHOUT END FOR THE ENTIRE FAMILY

The trees sold to plant after the holidays are hearty stock with the resilience to make the transfer from outdoors to inside and then back out again.

❧ Planning for a Living Tree

If the idea appeals to you, there are a few basics about the project. Plan to keep a living tree in your house for no longer than a week; any more time will tax its strength and stamina.

Consider the size of tree when it's full grown when you're choosing a location in the yard. Give it plenty of wide-open spreading space and room overhead to grow. Refer to the specifications on its ID tag so you won't plant it too close to the house or other trees and shrubbery.

When you're shopping, stand back and look at the tree. The foliage should be fresh and the tree should have a straight trunk and a well-balanced system of branches. A tree in a container should have moist soil, which you can feel if you dig down into it and feel its texture. A tree that's been grown in a field and then dug out and balled in burlap should be freshly dug and not wrapped too tightly with ropes. If fresh weeds or grass are growing out of the root ball, that tells you it's freshly cut and probably has a healthy root system. Avoid a tree with a broken root ball; it should be intact, not cracked or dried out.

If you live in an area where the ground freezes in December, dig the hole for the tree well before then. Dig the hole as deep as the root ball and at least twice as wide. If you are not sure of the size of the root ball visit the nursery where you plan to purchase your tree and take some measurements. To keep anyone from falling in the hole cover it with a sheet of old plywood or a row of 2 × 4s. Shovel the dirt from the hole into a wheelbarrow and store it in the garage or protect it with a covering so it doesn't freeze.

Before you bring a tree home decide where to store it before bringing it inside to be decorated. It should be kept in a protected, yet unheated holding place to make the transition from outdoors to inside. Be careful when handling the tree; it can be cumbersome but it is very delicate. If you have a small car, have the nursery deliver the tree, to lessen the risk of breaking branches or damaging the root ball in the transfer. An appliance dolly or a wheelbarrow can help you move it from the car or truck to its holding place.

The outdoors-to-indoors transition is not easy because a tree goes into its dormant stage in the fall. When brought inside a heated house there's a danger that it will break its dormancy and begin its growing cycle. Put it in an unheated porch or garage where it can adjust to its new environment and not be shocked by the transmission. Keep the soil moist and mist the needles so they don't dry out.

In the house, set up the tree for decorating in a wash tub or any large container that will hold it. Locate it near a window for light and far from a fireplace or heating system outlets. Decorate the tree with small twinkling lights instead of larger ones that create more heat and consequently dry it out. Even better, use flood lights on the floor to illuminate the tree laden with ornaments and garlands. Avoid using foil or plastic "icicle" strips because they are very difficult to remove. If decorations allow, mist the tree occasionally during the time it's indoors.

After Christmas, carefully move the tree to the hole that will be its permanent home. Remove the container or loosen the burlap around the root ball before gently easing the tree into the hole. Set it erect, and level with soil it is planted in. Fill in the hole with the original soil mixed with compost and topping soil. Don't pack the soil heavily with your feet; it's better to tamp with a rake or hoe. Water the hole and then smooth soil around the base of the tree. Cover the area with a layer of mulch. Don't forget to keep the soil moist throughout the winter months.

SECTION III

Easy Make and Build Projects

SOAKER HOSE

COMMERCIAL SOAKER HOSES ARE MORE EXPENSIVE THAN THE HOMEMADE TYPE, BUT NO MORE EFFICIENT

*D*on't throw away an old leaky hose; put it to good use by making it into a soaker hose. To do that, make small holes all along the length of the hose; they will allow a slow trickle of water to be released onto the ground wherever the hose runs. A soaker hose is a popular choice for gardeners who want to water their beds at a slow pace, without getting involved with an elaborate underground system. It is also the most efficient method of watering your garden because very little water evaporates into the air, as it does with a spray or sprinkler head.

❧ Planning the Project

Along with the old hose you need an in-line hose turn-off valve to screw onto one end, and a hose cap to seal off the other end. These parts are sold in home and garden centers in the hose departments. Before you go shopping, check the fittings at the ends of the old hose you plan to use.

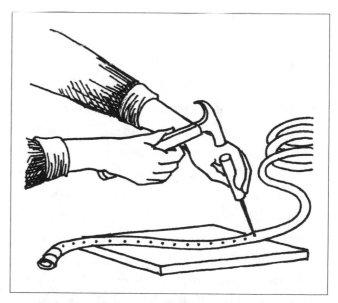

MAKING A SOAKER HOSE IS AN EXCELLENT WAY TO RECYCLE A LEAKY GARDEN HOSE

If they are cracked or bent out of shape, buy replacements.

❧ Step by Step

The job of making a soaker hose requires punching hundreds of small holes all along a garden hose. To make the holes you can use any sharp tool like an ice pick, an awl, a hammer and nail, or a $^1/_{16}$-inch bit in a hand or electric drill.

Put the hose on a piece of scrap wood and start poking holes. Space the holes 2 to 3 inches apart. You can make two holes at a time if you punch the tool all the way through the hose so it comes out the other side. The more holes, the better. Don't try to keep them in a straight line. Let the hose twist or turn as you work so that the holes will let water come out in all directions.

When you are finished making the holes, put the hose cap on one end and the in-line valve on the other end.

To install the soaker hose, close the in-line turn-off valve and attach it to a section of garden hose that is connected to a spigot. Turn the water on at the spigot, and then open the in-line valve at the soaker hose. Adjust the flow so that water dribbles out of all the soaker holes. If your soaker hose is long, water may squirt out of the holes nearest the valve when you open it enough to get water all the way to the other end. However, once the soaker hose is full of water you can usually adjust the in-line valve for a fairly even, slow flow all along the soaker hose. Once you have adjusted the in-line valve, leave it alone. Turn the water off and on at the spigot instead, so you won't have to adjust the valve every time you use it.

Soaker Hose Materials List

QUANTITY	SIZE	MATERIAL	PART
1	Hose fittings are either $^5/_8''$ or $^3/_4''$ diameter; get the size to match the hose you are using	Brass/plastic	In-line hose turn-off valve
1		Brass/plastic	Hose cap
1		Brass/plastic	Male hose end (optional)
1		Brass/plastic	Female hose end (optional)

KNEELING PAD/ SEAT

*A*nyone who spends more than an hour working in the garden will agree that kneeling in flower and vegetable beds can take a toll on your knees and joints. Gardening is wonderful exercise, but it should not be painful. To eliminate some of that strain on your knees, you can build a kneeling pad that does double duty as a little garden seat when it is designed around a standard foam kneeling pad that sells for a few dollars and is readily available in garden centers and hardware stores.

❧ Planning the Project

This project uses so little wood you may be able to build it from lumberyard scraps. Most yards have short cutoff pieces of 1 × 10 lumber lying around or in a scrap bin. Since the longest piece you need is less than 2 feet, look for scraps before purchasing a 6-foot length of 1 × 10. See the accompanying parts list for sizes. The cleats and brace can be cut from 1 × 10 stock, or from 1 × 2 furring stock.

If you can't find a rubber kneeling pad close to

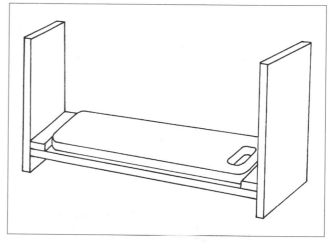

KNEELING PAD/SEAT

Kneeling Pad/Seat Materials List

QUANTITY	SIZE★	MATERIAL
1	1″ × 10″ × 6′	#2 pine
1	8″ × 19″	Foam pad
1 box	4d	Aluminum finishing nails
1 box	2½″	Galvanized all-purpose screws
1	Small container	Carpenter's glue

Kneeling Pad/Seat Parts List

PART	NUMBER	SIZE★	MATERIAL
Side	2	¾″ × 9¼″ × 13½″	Pine
Base	1	¾″ × 9¼″ × 22″	Pine
Cleat	2	¾″ × 1½″ × 9¼″	Pine
Brace	1	¾″ × 1½″ × 22″	Pine

★ Sizes in the Parts List are actual dimensions; lumber sizes in the Materials List are nominal (stock) dimensions.

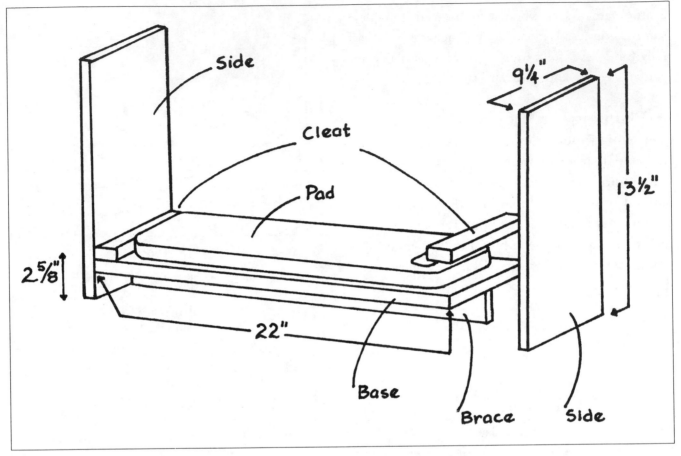

KNEELING PAD/SEAT PARTS AND ASSEMBLY

the dimensions of the base, choose a larger size pad and cut it to fit.

❧ Step by Step

Since this project has so few parts, the cutting and assembly are easy. Cut the base, two cleats, and the brace to length. Draw a line down the center of the base. Start four evenly spaced 4d finishing nails through the base along this line.

Coat one long edge of the brace with glue and align it under the nails. Check that its ends are flush with the ends of the base. Then drive the nails into the brace.

Now use 4d finishing nails and carpenter's glue to fasten the cleats across the ends of the base. Make them flush with the ends of the base, on the opposite side from the brace, as illustrated.

There can be considerable pressure applied to the sides when you push against them as you get up from a kneeling position. To attach the sides securely to the base, use 2-inch galvanized all-purpose screws instead of nails. These screws require a screwdriver with a Phillips head tip. If you have a variable-speed electric drill, purchase a Phillips head tip to fit the drill and use it as a power screwdriver. Drive the screws into the edges of the cleats, not into the ends of the base, for the best holding power.

To help align the screws, draw a straight line across each side 2⅝ inches up from the bottom edge. This will place the screws in the center of the cleat and keep the brace flush with the bottom of the side. Drill four evenly spaced ⅛-inch pilot holes through the side along the layout line. Then insert the screws into the pilot holes in each side and tighten them until their tips start to protrude from the backside of the board.

At one end of the seat, apply glue to the ends of the base and brace and to the edge of the cleat. Place one side against the end of the base and align it so that its bottom is flush with the brace and its sides are flush with the edges of the base. Then drive the screws all the way into the wood. Drill two pilot holes completely through the side aligned with the end of the brace. Then insert the screws into the holes and drive them through the side and into the end of the brace. Repeat this process to attach the side piece at the other end of the seat.

SIMPLE TRELLIS

A trellis provides an attractive vertical support for climbing vines and flowers, which can be a colorful coverup or enhancement in a yard. Planted with a cascade of morning glories it will conceal an unsightly garage wall or call attention to an area with its bountiful blooms.

Our curved trellis is easier to build than you might expect because it is constructed of five pieces of wood lattice spread open like a fan. The slats are held open by a crosstree dowel that fits

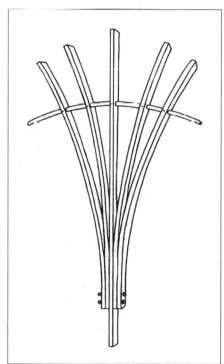

FAN–SHAPED TRELLIS

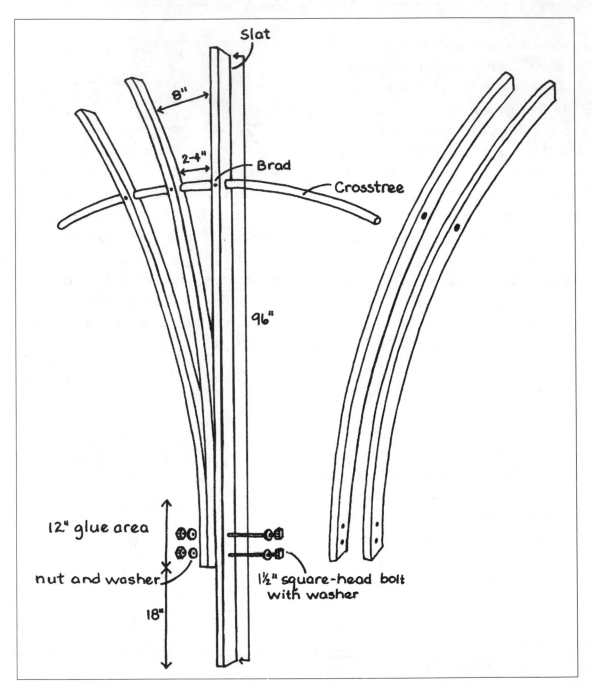

Slat

8"

2-4"

Brad

Crosstree

96"

12" glue area

nut and washer

1½" square-head bolt
with washer

18"

TRELLIS ASSEMBLY

through holes drilled in the slats near the top.

The center slat of the trellis extends at the bottom to act as a mounting stake, which makes it easy to place the trellis next to a wall or fence. Since the trellis is so lightweight it can also be fastened to the back of a wooden potting box or the framework of a raised bed (see pages 125–127).

❧ Planning the Project

This project relies on the flexibility of the lattice strips since its fan shape requires bending. Different woods have different bending characteristics. Redwood and cedar are the best choice because they are very flexible and are weather resistant. Pine lattice can also be used but pine is not very rot resistant. Pine will hold up fairly well if painted but redwood or cedar can be left natural and will be virtually maintenance free.

The material list calls for 8-foot sections of lattice since most lumberyards stock lattice in this length. If possible purchase one 8-foot section to make the center slat and four 72-inch pieces to make the outer slats.

❧ Step by Step

This trellis is very easy to build. It is constructed from $1^1/8$-inch lattice and a $3/8$-inch dowel. Cut the four outer slats to length then cut the center slat to length if it is over 8 feet long. Be careful, lattice is light and easy to work but it can be fragile. Place the slats on edge with the long slat

Trellis Parts List

PART	NUMBER	SIZE	MATERIAL
Slat	5	$1/4'' \times$ $1^1/8'' \times 96''$	Lattice
Crosstree	1	$3/8'' \times 36''$	Dowel

Trellis Materials List

QUANTITY	SIZE	MATERIAL
5	$1^1/8'' \times 8'$	Lattice
1	$3/8'' \times 3'$	Dowel
1 box	$1''$	Wire brads
2 each	$1/4'' \times 1^1/2''$	Galvanized bolts, nuts, washers
1	Small container	Waterproof glue

★ Sizes in the Parts List are actual dimensions; lumber sizes in the Materials List are nominal (stock) dimensions.

in the middle on a flat surface. Align their top ends. Measure up 12 inches from the bottom ends of the short pieces and draw a pencil line across the entire bundle. Also mark the long center slat where the short slats end.

Unbundle the lattice and apply waterproof glue to their broad faces between the layout marks. Reassemble the slats, checking that they are aligned at the top and that the longest slat is in the center. Clamp the slats together and set them aside until the glue dries. If you do not have a clamp, bind the glued section together with twine.

The base of the trellis is reinforced with two 1/4-inch-diameter bolts. Drill a 1/4-inch hole for one of these bolts 3 inches above the bottom of the short slats and another hole 6 inches above the first. To protect the soft wood, slip a washer on each bolt, push the bolts through their holes, slip on second washers, and thread on the nuts. Finger-tighten the nuts first; when snug, tighten them firmly with a wrench or pair of pliers.

The crosstree dowel spreads the slats. It is installed about a foot from the top of the trellis. Drill a 3/8-inch-diameter hole through the center of the slat sides 12 inches down from the top of the bundle. Then insert the dowel into the hole and center the slat bundle on the dowel. Drill a 1/16-inch pilot hole through the edge of the long center slat and into the dowel. Then drive a 1-inch wire brad through the slat into the dowel to secure it.

Cut an 8-inch spacer from a piece of lattice scrap. Then spread one of the slats next to the center slat by pulling its end to one side. Slip the spacer between the two slats and push it down between the slats until it rests on the crosstree dowel. With the spacer in this position the slats are spread apart 8 inches. Drill a pilot hole through the edge of the slat and into the dowel and fasten the slat to the dowel with a brad just as you did with the center slat.

Repeat the process with the slat on the other side of the center slat to keep the bending forces evenly distributed. As you spread the slats, help the dowel bend into a slight arc by pulling gently down on its ends. Spread and fasten the remaining slats.

After all four slats are spread and nailed in place, cut off the ends of the crosstree dowel about 1 inch beyond each outside slat. Cut the bottom of the center slat into a point and your trellis is ready to be planted in the yard.

BIRD FEEDER

A bird feeder is a reminder to feathered friends that they're welcome in your garden. By attracting birds to your yard you'll enjoy hearing their chirps and chatter and appreciate their appetites. They gobble up insects and pests that damage plants, making their presence in your yard a double treat.

To encourage birds to visit your garden build this bird feeder and keep it freshly stocked. It's easy to build and features a lift-off hatch at the top to make replenishing the feeder a simple job.

❧ Planning the Project
This project does not require large pieces of wood so you can probably purchase some cutoff

scraps from your local lumberyard. Cedar is the best choice for appearance and durability. With the exception of the plastic bin sides, all the parts can be cut from standard-size lumber.

The hatch parts are 1½ inches wide so you may have to cut them from wider stock if your lumberyard does not carry 1 × 2 cedar stock. The bin sides are made from clear plastic. Purchase acrylic plastic, which is easy to cut, instead of polycarbonate such as Lexan™, which is more expensive and more difficult to cut.

❧ Step by Step

Cut the feeder and bin ends first. To lay out a feeder end, cut a piece of 1 × 8 stock 9 inches long. Measure the width at one end, divide that in half, and mark the center of the piece. Then measure down 3⅝ inches along one edge from that end and mark the spot. Do the same on opposite edge (see detail). Connect these points with the center point at the end, cut along the lines, and discard the triangular corner pieces. Lay out and cut the other feeder end in the same way.

To make a bin end, cut a piece 5⅜ inches long from 1 × 8 stock. Then find the center of the board at one end (as you did when laying out the feeder end) and mark it. Then measure from this center mark ¾ inch to each side and mark those points. You now have two marks 1½ inches apart in the center of the board at one end.

Connect these points to the corners at the

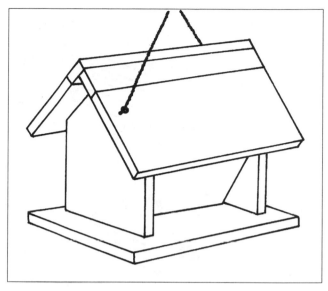

BIRD FEEDER

other end of the board (see detail). Cut along these layout lines and discard the triangular pieces. You have a trapezoid-shaped bin end. Cut a second bin end in the same way.

Use waterproof glue and 3d aluminum finishing nails to attach each bin end to a feeder end. Note that the narrow end of the bin end goes down, flush with the bottom of the feeder end. Set these assemblies aside for the glue to dry.

Cut the bottom to length from 1 × 10 stock and the roof parts from 1 × 6 stock. Cut the hatch parts from 1 × 2 stock. All are 12 inches long. Cut two bin sides from ⅛-inch clear plastic sheeting such as Plexiglas.™ This material isn't hard to cut with a fine-tooth saw but it is easier to cut if you score the surface and then break the plastic sheet over the edge of a table. To do this,

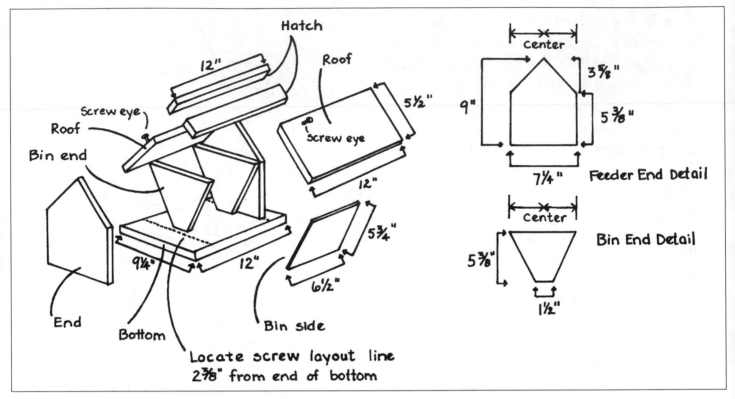

BIRD FEEDER PARTS AND ASSEMBLY

place a straightedge next to the cut line and score the plastic sheeting with a sharp utility knife several times. Then align the score with the edge of a table and push smartly on the overhanging piece to break it off. Each side is $6^1/2 \times 5^3/4$ inches.

Next, mark the bottom and drill pilot holes for screws that will hold the feeder ends. Measure in $2^3/8$ inches from each end and draw straight lines across the width of the bottom. Measure in $2^1/2$ inches from each side edge of the bottom along both lines and make marks at these four points.

Also make a mark on each line exactly in the center of the width. Drill a $1/8$-inch-diameter pilot hole through these six marks.

Now drill $1/4$-inch-diameter pilot holes in the corners of the plastic bin sides. Locate each hole $1/2$ inch in from its long (top or bottom) edge and $3/8$ inch in from its side edge. Drill matching pilot holes in the edges of the bin ends. To locate these holes, put the bin side on the bin end and align their top edges. Note that the bottom of the bin side stops short of the bottom of the bin end, leaving a space for birdseed to drop out. Mark the hole locations on the bin ends and drill pilot holes about $1/2$ inch deep. Fasten the bin sides to the end assemblies with $3/4$-inch-long **#**6 brass round head (RH) screws. Don't overtighten the screws or you may crack the plastic. This is the bin assembly.

Attach the bin assembly to the bottom with waterproof glue and $1^5/8$-inch galvanized all-purpose screws. These screws require a screwdriver with a Phillips tip. Place the assembly on the bottom with its ends centered over the pilot holes in the bottom. Each feeder end will be 2 inches from its end of the bottom. Run a pencil along the joint between the end and bottom to make a light mark you can use for alignment during final assembly. That way you won't get glue all over the bottom.

To make final assembly easier hold the bin assembly in place on the bottom and use a nail or a pencil to mark the hole locations on the bottom edges of the feeder ends. Remove the bin assembly and drill pilot holes at the marked points on the ends.

Apply glue to the bottom edges of the feeder and bin ends, then place the assembly on the bottom. Install the screws from underneath the bottom and tighten them to pull the parts together.

Glue and nail the two hatch pieces together with 3d aluminum nails. Place the hatch on top of the feeder ends and mark where the bottom edges are. Cut two roof pieces 12 inches long from 1 × 6 lumber. Apply glue to the top edges

Bird Feeder Parts List			
PART	NUMBER	SIZE*	MATERIAL
Bottom	1	$3/4'' \times$ $9^1/4'' \times 12''$	Cedar
End	2	$3/4'' \times$ $7^1/4'' \times 9''$	Cedar
Bin end	2	$3/4'' \times$ $7^1/4'' \times 5^3/8''$	Cedar
Roof	2	$3/4'' \times$ $5^1/2'' \times 12''$	Cedar
Hatch	2	$3/4'' \times$ $1^1/2'' \times 12''$	Cedar
Bin side	2	$1/8'' \times$ $5^3/4'' \times 6^1/2''$	Plastic

of the feeder ends below the hatch edges and place the roof pieces in position. Center them so there is a 2-inch overhang at each end and nail them in place with 3d aluminum finishing nails. Since the hatch pieces are the same width and are nailed together they form a hatch with one side $3/4$ inch longer than the other. If you want the feeder to have equal overhangs, trim $3/4$ inch off one roof panel. Remove the hatch so it is not glued in place by stray glue that may be pushed out of the end–roof joint.

Install the screweyes for hanging the feeder 1 inch down from the upper edge of the roof. Drill pilot holes. Each screweye should go through the roof and into the top edge of the feeder end. You can start the screweye by hand, but turning will

Bird Feeder Materials List

QUANTITY	SIZE★	MATERIAL	PART
1	1″ × 12″ × 1′	Cedar	Bottom
1	1″ × 10″ × 1′	Cedar	Feeder ends/Bin ends
1	1″ × 6″ × 1′	Cedar	Roof
1	1″ × 2″ × 2′	Cedar	Hatch
1	⅛″ × 5¾″ × 13″	Clear plastic	Bin sides
1	Small container	Waterproof glue	
1 box	3d	Aluminum finishing nails	
8	#6	Brass round head wood screws	
8	1⅝″	Galvanized all-purpose screws	
2	1¼″	Zinc-plated screweyes	

★ Sizes in the Parts List are actual dimensions; lumber sizes in the Materials List are nominal (stock) dimensions.

get hard so put a nail or screwdriver shaft through the eye to give you leverage to screw it all the way down until the eye touches the roof. Install the screweyes at opposite ends of the feeder, on opposite sides of other roof.

Hang your feeder from an 18-inch-long piece of light rope. Tie the ends to the screweyes, then tie a loop in the center of the rope. With the screweyes offset on opposite sides of the roof, the feeder will be more stable when you hang it from a tree.

We have had no problems with squirrels getting into the feeder. If you have a very smart squirrel in your yard, you might have to install a lock on the hatch. An easy to open turnbutton used to hold storm windows in place screwed to the roof will keep the hatch locked against even the most persistent invaders.

PLANT CONTAINER

Do you want to dress up an unattractive plant container or tie a group of mismatched ones together? The plant container or planter box in this project will conceal one or more not-so-pretty containers, showcasing blooms and foliage instead. It is bottomless, so when used outdoors on a deck or patio water can drain out the bottom. (Large containers with bottoms are heavy to move and often are damaged when water settles and puddles inside.) The parts are easy to cut out, and you can build the container in a short time.

❧ Planning the Project

If you plan to use your planter box outside and minimum maintenance is your goal, choose a weather-resistant wood like redwood, cedar, or pressure-treated lumber. Of course, if the planter box is to be used in a protected area just about any variety of wood will do. A couple of coats of paint will also protect less weather-resistant woods like pine, but any painted surface left outside will eventually need maintenance.

Assembly of this box is easy, but there are quite a few boards to cut. None of the cuts is complex, so you can do the job with a crosscut handsaw if you are feeling energetic. A handheld jig saw (saber saw) or circular saw will do all the cutting in short order. Or you may want to have the lumberyard cut the parts to length; check what the cutting charge is before you decide.

Since moisture is present in clay pots and soil, use galvanized or aluminum nails to assemble this project even if you don't plan to put your container outside.

❧ Step by Step

Cutting the side boards to length is straightforward. Lay out the lengths on 1 × 4 stock and make accurate cuts. One end of each board will be visible and all must be the same length, so precision is important. Then cut four corner posts to length from the 2 × 2 stock.

Assembly of the planter sides is easy. Glue and nail the left ends of four side boards to a corner

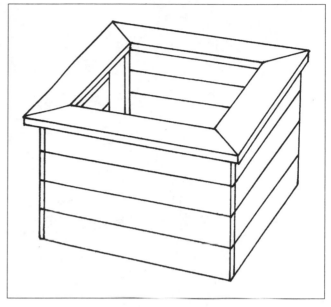

PLANT CONTAINER

post. Be sure the ends are flush with the side of the corner post and that the top and bottom boards are flush with the ends of the post. Also check that the side boards are square with the corner post so the planter box will be square. Glue and nail the other three sides in the same way, with the corner post at the same end in each assembly.

To assemble the planter box, the end without a corner post of each assembly will overlap the corner post and side board ends on the adjacent side. Apply glue to the face of the corner post and ends of the side boards on one assembly, then position a second side assembly so its side boards overlap and are flush with the outside of first as-

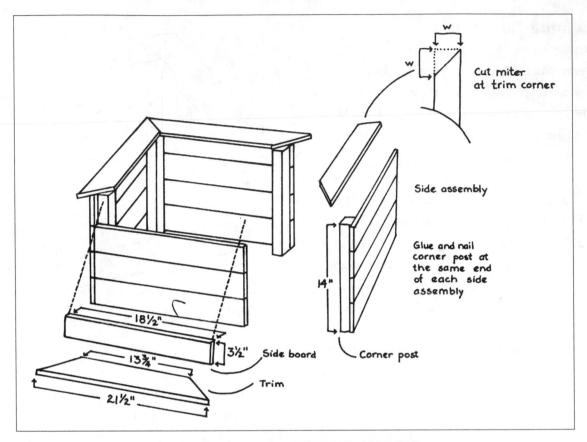

Cut miter at trim corner

Side assembly

Glue and nail corner post at the same end of each side assembly

14"

18½"

3½"

Side board

13¾"

Corner post

Trim

21½"

PLANT CONTAINER PARTS AND ASSEMBLY

sembly. Then nail these side boards to the corner post. Don't drive the nails too close to the end or you may split the wood. And take care to align the nails and space them evenly.

Set this assembly upright on a flat surface and use a carpenter's square to check that they form a 90-degree angle at the corner. Also check that the bottom edges are in contact with the flat surface they rest on, to assure that the sides are straight.

Join the remaining side assemblies in the same way, fastening them all together to form a box. Check the box for squareness with the carpenter's square. You can also check for squareness by measuring the distance between both pairs of diagonally opposite corners. If the measurements are the same, the box is square.

After the glue has dried, which takes several hours, cut and fit the trim pieces for the top edges. They have mitered joints at the corner.

The easiest way to make these parts is to first cut the 1 × 4 boards to the length of the longest edge, then cut 45-degree miters on the ends. A detail in the illustration shows how to mark the cut line by measuring the width of board. Make the cut so the point of the miter is exactly at the end of the board.

Place the trim pieces in position on the top of the box and arrange them so that the mitered corners match. To mark a line for nailing, measure from the outside edge of each trim piece to the face of the top side board. Add $3/8$ inch and transfer the measurement to the top face of the trim piece. Do this at each end, then draw a line between the two marks—it will correspond to the center line of the edge of the side board that the trim piece rests on. Drive 4d finishing nails along this line every 4 inches. Attach the other trim pieces in the same way.

Hold each miter joint together with a 4d nail driven through the edge of the boards about an inch from their ends. Angle the nail so it runs at a right angle across the joint line. To prevent the wood from splitting, drill a pilot hole through the first trim piece. If you don't have a small bit ($1/16$ inch diameter), cut off the head of a finishing nail and use the nail shank as a bit in your drill.

Plant Container Parts List

PART	NUMBER	SIZE★	MATERIAL
Side	16	$3/4'' \times 3^{1}/_{2}'' \times 18^{1}/_{2}''$	Redwood
Trim	4	$3/4'' \times 3^{1}/_{2}'' \times 21^{1}/_{2}''$	Redwood
Corner post	4	$1^{1}/_{2}'' \times 1^{1}/_{2}'' \times 14''$	Redwood

Plant Container Materials List

QUANTITY	SIZE★	MATERIAL
5	$1'' \times 4'' \times 8'$	Redwood
1	$2'' \times 2'' \times 6'$	Redwood
1 box	4d	Finishing nails ★★
1 box	6d	Finishing nails ★★
1	8-oz. container	Carpenter's glue

★ Sizes in the Parts List are actual dimensions; lumber sizes in the Materials List are nominal (stock) dimensions.
★★ Aluminum or galvanized.

EASY BENCH

*T*his garden bench will fit in just about any backyard. It might provide a place to sit and watch the children play, or maybe it will be a favorite resting spot in a quiet part of the yard. A

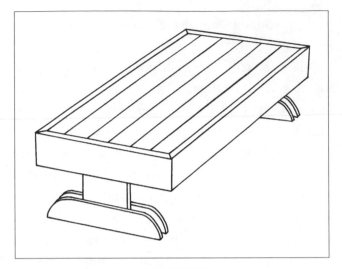

EASY BENCH

PART	NUMBER	SIZE★	MATERIAL
Seat board	5	$1^1/_2'' \times$ $3^1/_2'' \times 48''$	Redwood
Side trim	2	$1^1/_2'' \times$ $5^1/_2'' \times 51''$	Redwood
End trim	2	$1^1/_2'' \times$ $5^1/_2'' \times$ $21^1/_2''$	Redwood
Leg	2	$1^1/_2'' \times$ $7^1/_4'' \times$ $14^1/_4''$	Redwood
Filler block	4	$1^1/_2'' \times$ $3^1/_2'' \times 3^1/_2''$	Redwood
Top support	4	$^3/_4'' \times$ $3^1/_2'' \times$ $18^1/_2''$	Redwood
Foot	4	$^3/_4'' \times$ $3^1/_2'' \times$ $18^1/_2''$	Redwood

Easy Bench Parts List

★ Sizes in the Parts List are actual dimensions; lumber sizes in the Materials List are nominal (stock) dimensions.

bench can be attractive on a breezeway to display potted plants, or as seating on a patio or deck.

Since you can build this bench with basic tools, it's a good choice for a first-time wood-worker. After you've built one, you might even decide to make a second one!

❧ Planning the Project

A piece of outdoor furniture is best made from heavy stock so it is sturdy and solid. This bench uses mostly 2 × 4 and 2 × 6 dimensional lumber. For a finished appearance the outside trim pieces can be joined with mitered corners. However, cutting vertically through a 2 × 6 at a 45-degree angle requires care; any miscuts or variations will show up in the joint. Many lumberyards will make the 45-degree cuts for you. Or you may choose to have square corners, as shown in de-

tail in the assembly illustration. In either case, check the inside dimensions of the trim assembly after the pieces are cut. Put the four parts together and measure the inside width and length between opposite trim pieces. When you cut the top supports, make them exactly that width to ensure that the end trim pieces will fit side trim when the bench is assembled. Cut the

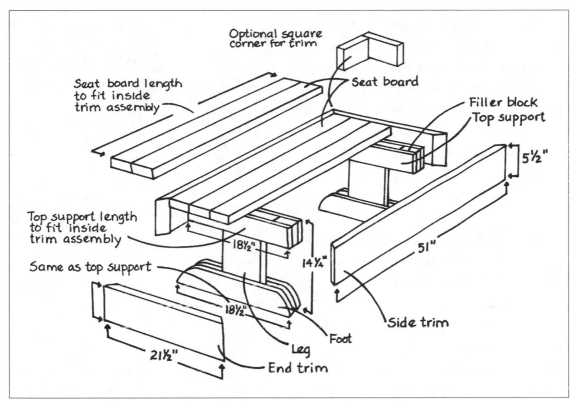

Optional square
corner for trim

Seat board

Seat board length
to fit inside
trim assembly

Filler block
Top support

5½"

Top support length
to fit inside
trim assembly

51"

Same as top support

18½"

14¼"

Side trim

18½"

Foot

21½"

Leg

End trim

BENCH PARTS AND ASSEMBLY

seat boards to the inside length of the trim assembly.

For the best holding power, use all-purpose galvanized 2- and 3-inch screws. These screws require a screwdriver with a Phillips head tip. Phillips hand screwdrivers are inexpensive. If you have a variable-speed electric drill, you can purchase a Phillips head bit that allows you to use the drill as a power screwdriver. Set the screw heads just below the surface of the wood but don't drive them in too deeply because the small depression left in the head will collect water and

promote rot. If you prefer, you can substitute 16d and 8d galvanized nails for the screws.

🍃 Step by Step

Assemble the legs first. Cut the top supports and feet from 1 × 4 stock. They are all the same length—the inside width of the trim assembly, as explained earlier. The top corners of the feet are rounded. Lay out the cutting lines with a pencil and a piece of string or a compass. To draw the arc at one end, mark a point 3½ inches from the end of the board on its lower edge. Tie the string around the pencil. Hold the pencil point at the bottom corner and pull string taut to the mark on the edge of the board. Swing the pencil upward to draw an arc from the lower edge to the top edge. If you use a compass place its point at the mark and extend the pencil to the end of the board and make the arc. Mark the other end of the foot in the same way.

Use a coping or hand-held jig saw (saber saw) to cut along these arcs. Then use the first foot as a pattern to mark the other three. When they are all cut, clamp them together and smooth any rough edges with sandpaper.

Cut the two legs from 2 × 8 stock. Then install the top supports flush with the top of the leg and the feet flush with the bottom of the leg. Before fastening these parts with 2-inch screws, make sure that they are perpendicular to the legs.

Cut the seat boards from 2 × 4 stock. Their length should be the same as the inside dimension of the trim assembly, as explained earlier. Cut the filler blocks that go between the top supports from the same stock. Install the filler blocks between the top supports so there is solid wood to screw the side trim and seat boards to.

First install the outer seat boards. Place the leg assemblies on a flat surface and place a seat board across them at one edge. The legs are positioned 4½ inches from the ends of the seat board, and the seat board must be flush with the ends of the top supports. Use 3-inch screws to attach the seat

Easy Bench Materials List

QUANTITY	SIZE★	MATERIAL	PART
1	2″ × 6″ × 10′	Redwood	Side trim
1	2″ × 6″ × 6′	Redwood	End trim
3	2″ × 4″ × 8′	Redwood	Seat board
1	2″ × 8″ × 4′	Redwood	Leg
2	1″ × 4″ × 8′	Redwood	Top support/Foot
1 box	3″ or 16d	All-purpose galvanized screws Galvanized nails	
1 box	2″ or 8d	All-purpose galvanized screws Galvanized nails	

board. After checking alignment, drive one screw through the seat board into the filler block between the top supports of each leg assembly.

Place a second seat board in position flush with the ends of the top supports on the other side of the bench. Check alignment, then install the second seat board with one screw in each filler block. Now install the rest of the seat boards. Tack a piece of scrap across the ends of the outside seat boards as an alignment guide for positioning the other seat boards. Lay them in position and adjust them for equal spaces between all the boards, about ¼ inch. You will find it easier to maintain this spacing if you place a screw or other spacer between the boards and work from the outside in. Install each board with just one screw into the filler block at each end. When all the boards are in place, drive additional screws so that each board is held by two screws into each leg assembly.

Now install the trim, the side pieces first. The inside of the miter cut (or the square-cut ends) should align with the ends of the seat boards and the top edges should be flush with the tops of the seat boards. Screw the side trim to the filler blocks which are sandwiched between the top supports with 3-inch screws.

Finally, screw the end trim piece to the ends of the seat boards with 3-inch screws. After they are in place, fasten the miter joints together with a couple of 2-inch screws. These screws are near the ends of the boards, so to prevent splitting the wood first drill a ⅛-inch pilot hole for each screw. The hole only has to go through the miter.

Redwood is naturally weather resistant, but to keep its new look apply several coats of a waterproofing sealer. This clear finish will seal the wood pores and prevent dirt and grime from dulling the appearance of the wood. At least once a year scrub the bench clean and reapply a coat of sealer; your bench will look great for years to come.

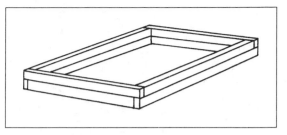

FRAME FOR RAISED GARDEN BED

RAISED GARDEN

T alk to anyone who has made the switch to a raised garden and you're likely to be listening to a convert. By enclosing and raising a bed for flowers or vegetables you can work in the garden more easily. The soil, nutrients, and compost materials are contained, so cultivating is less tiresome. You'll use less water in a raised bed, and if you're unhappy with the amount of sun or the crop yield, you can move a raised bed to another location. You can also expand a raised bed by building onto the original structure, or reshape it by reusing the original building materials.

❧ Planning the Project
This is a very easy project to build, but it is made from heavy 4 × 4 timbers, so you will probably need a helper to heft the lumber around your yard. The materials are much too heavy to transport in the trunk or on top of your car, so arrange to have the timbers and soil delivered.

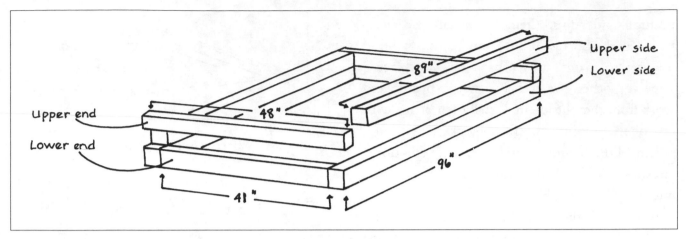

RAISED GARDEN FRAME ASSEMBLY

Since the framework for the bed sits directly on the ground it must be made from durable wood. Pressure-treated wood made for direct contact with the ground is your best choice. When working with pressure-treated wood remember that the chemicals that preserve the wood are also toxic. Wear gloves and wash your hands after handling pressure-treated wood. Wear a dust mask to protect yourself from inhaling sawdust while cutting this material and wash your work clothes separately from the regular laundry. Don't dispose of pressure-treated lumber scraps by burning.

If you plan to use the raised bed to grow vegetables, line the sides of the framework with heavy plastic before filling it with soil, to prevent any preservatives impregnated in the wood from leaching out and being absorbed by your plants.

Tack a 2-foot-wide strip of plastic to the inside of the frame, but don't totally cover the ground at the bottom or you will prevent proper drainage.

Before you begin construction of a raised bed, turn over the soil in the area where it will be located, then build the framework in place. Even though the bed is small, it will require about 15 cubic feet of new soil to fill it up so consider having the soil delivered with the timbers.

❧ Step by Step

This is an easy building project because only a few parts need to be cut to length. The lower sides are two full-length 8-foot 4 × 4 timber. The upper sides are cut from two full-length 4 × 4s. To make the ends, cut two full-length 4 × 4s in half, and then trim two of those pieces to make the lower ends. This job will be much easier if you have a circular saw; cutting 4 × 4 timbers with a hand saw will work up a good sweat. If you want to use a hand saw choose a bow saw, usually used for pruning trees and cutting firewood. Pilot holes make driving the large spikes used to hold the timbers together easy. Since the timbers are thicker than standard drill bits purchase a 6-inch-long ³/₁₆-inch electrician's drill bit. These bits are used to drill through walls and floors to install phone wires and are carried by most home centers.

Begin assembly of the raised bed by placing lower side pieces in position along the outside edge of the soil bed you turned over. Then place the lower end pieces between the sides and square up the frame. Measure between pairs of diagonally opposite corners and compare the measurements. If they are the same, the frame is square.

Place the upper ends in position, then put the upper sides in place between them. Recheck the bed for squareness. Use a long ³/₁₆-inch drill bit to bore two pilot holes completely through the upper end and into the lower side about an inch. Then drill similar pilot holes in the other three corners and drive 40d galvanized spikes through these holes. A small 3-lb. sledgehammer will make driving the spikes easier.

Drill pilot holes about 6 inches from each end of the upper side timbers. Then drive spikes into these holes. Drill another set of pilot holes in the center of both the upper ends and upper sides,

then drive spikes into these holes. Drill additional pilot holes in the upper side between each center and end spike and drive spikes through them.

Make sure that all nail heads are driven below the surface of the timbers so there is no danger of catching your clothes or scraping hands or legs on them. Staple plastic to the inside of the timbers if you are using pressure-treated wood and plan to grow vegetables in this bed.

Garden Frame Parts List

PART	NUMBER	SIZE*	MATERIAL**
Upper side	2	3¹/₂″ × 3¹/₂″ × 89″	PT wood
Upper end	2	3¹/₂″ × 3¹/₂″ × 48″	PT wood
Lower side	2	3¹/₂″ × 3¹/₂″ × 96″	PT wood
Lower end	2	3¹/₂″ × 3¹/₂″ × 41″	PT wood

Garden Frame Materials List

QUANTITY	SIZE*	MATERIAL
6	4″ × 4″ × 8′	PT wood
1 box	40d	Galvanized nails
1	8′ × 9′	Heavy plastic sheeting

* Sizes in the Parts List are actual dimensions; lumber sizes in the Materials List are nominal (stock) sizes.
** PT: pressure-treated.

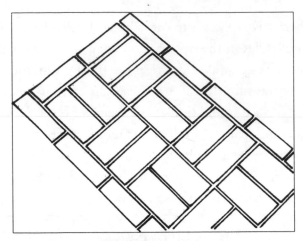

BRICK GARDEN PATH

BRICK GARDEN PATH

*T*he work involved in constructing a brick path through your garden will be repaid with years of enjoyment. Bricks are an attractive surface, not to mention a tough, durable material that will last a long time. They're ageless in design and proven to withstand temperature extremes. As a classic paving material bricks are attractive in a traditional garden or a contemporary landscape.

Do-it-yourself helpers like plastic grid trays, which take the guesswork out of brick alignment. These inexpensive grids are available at most large home centers and lumberyards or wherever paving materials are sold. They also help retard weed growth.

❧ Planning the Project

The materials for this project will build a straight path 21 inches wide and 10 feet long. If your needs are different use the techniques described here and purchase more or less materials. You will need $4^{1}/_{2}$ bricks for each square foot of pathway, and $1^{1}/_{2}$ bricks for each running foot of edging along each side and at the ends of the path. Bricks are $3^{3}/_{4}$ inches $\times 8$ inches $\times 2^{1}/_{4}$ inches. Brick edging is usually laid lengthwise, on the narrow edge. Choose paving bricks or bricks rated SW (severe weather) for a path.

Even a rather short path requires quite a pile of bricks and sand, so plan to have the materials delivered to your house and placed as close to the work site as possible. You will need a wheelbarrow or heavy-duty garden cart to move the excavated dirt from the path site. In addition you will need some 10-foot-long 2×2s as forms to help lay out the project. You can use old lumber or purchase the cheapest grade straight boards. You will also need some stakes. Cut them from 2×2 scrap or purchase a package of stakes, available at most lumberyards and home centers. Even though the assembled materials to build your

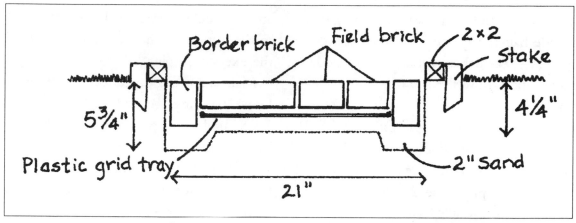

SET BRICKS ON A 2″ BED OF SAND AND FLUSH WITH THE SURROUNDING LAWN

walk can be intimidating, the bricks are laid one at a time.

You will have to remove 4 to 5 inches of sod and soil, so figure out where you will put it. Sod can be transplanted to some other part of your yard. The soil underneath can go into the garden or be spread in low areas around your property.

❧ Step by Step

Laying out this project is not difficult, but it is important that the walk be smooth. Bricks are 2¼ inches thick and they should be set on at least a 2-inch sand base. That means you must create a trench that is at least 4¼ inches deep in the center. The edges of the trench must be slightly deeper to accommodate the border bricks

which are laid on their side. Dig the edges of the trench 5¾ inches deep. If you dig a little too deep, fill the low areas with sand.

The overall width of the walk is 21 inches,

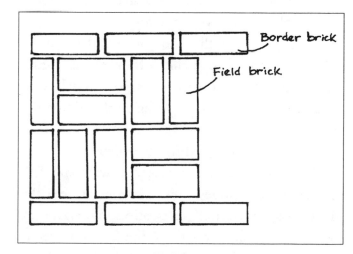

BRICK BASKET-WEAVE PATTERN

made up of bricks laid in a plastic grid tray in a 16-inch-wide half-basket-weave pattern between brick borders 2¼ inches wide on each side. These dimensions allow for a ¼-inch joint between bricks.

To lay out the walk use simple forms of 2 × 2 lumber placed along the edges of the walk. Cut some stakes and nail them to each end of the 2 × 2 boards. Then place the 2 × 2s in position along the edges of the walk. Drive the stakes into the ground until the form sits on the ground. Check the distance between the forms, especially in the center, and drive additional stakes to hold the forms a consistent 21 inches apart.

With a garden spade remove the sod from between the forms. Cut along the inside edges of the forms and across the width to divide the sod into 2-foot squares. Then work the blade of the spade under the sod to cut its roots. Remove the sod squares and put them in a shady place. Then dig out the soil between the forms. Sod is usually a couple of inches thick so you only have to remove 2 to 3 more inches of soil. The edging bricks are placed on their sides, so you will need a slightly deeper trench along each side of the walk.

Remove the soil and sod to a depth of at least 4¼ inches in the center of the walk and 5¾ inches along its edges, for the borders. Check the depth of the trench excavation by placing a straight piece of wood across the forms and measuring down from its bottom edge. The forms are 1½ inches high, so the actual measurement to the bottom of the trench will be the depth of the excavation plus 1½ inches.

Make a leveling board to smooth the sand bed. Use a straight piece of 2 × 2 stock and a piece of 1 × 8 lumber or plywood scrap. Cut the 2 × 2 long enough to bridge the forms and cut the 1 × 8 lumber to the width of the trench. Place the 2 × 2 across the trench on top of the forms, then nail the 1 × 8 lumber to it so the lower edge of the 1 × 8 is 2 inches from the bottom of the border trenches along each side.

Fill the entire trench with sand until it is about 3¾ inches from the top of the trench. Then drag the leveling board down the forms to scrape the sand to a uniform depth. Compact the sand in the border trenches with the end of a 2 × 4 or other board and add more sand where necessary. Then use the leveling board again to smooth the sand.

Place the border bricks on edge along one end of the trench first then along its sides. It is easier to place the border bricks at the other end of the path after the field bricks are set. After the border bricks are in place put a 2-foot piece of 2 × 2 stock on top of them and tap on it to drive any high bricks into the sand so they all are at the same depth. Fill any gaps between the bricks and the outside edge of the trench with sand. Now fill the trench with another inch of sand and compact it across the width between the side borders.

| Brick Garden Path Materials List ||
QUANTITY	MATERIAL
120	Paving bricks
4	80 lb. bag sand (1 bag/5 sq. ft. of path)
3	2 × 2 pine furring
8	2 × 2 stakes
7	Plastic grid trays

Remove the 1 × 8 board from the 2 × 2 leveling board and renail it so that it is 2¹/₄ inches (thickness of the bricks) below the top of the border bricks. Rest the leveling board on top of the forms and drag it down the trench to smooth the sand. You might have to add some sand if it does not come up to the level of the board. Test the level of the sand for the field bricks by placing a brick on the sand next to the edge bricks. It should be level or slightly higher but not lower than the border bricks. When the sand is level, place a plastic grid tray in the trench and lay bricks in place in it. Check the height of the bricks in the field with the 2 × 2 you used to tap the edge bricks. Place the 2 × 2 on the bricks and check that it touches the edge bricks on both sides. It is OK if the center bricks are slightly high because that promotes good drainage, but the field bricks should not be lower than the border bricks because water and snow will collect there.

Position the remaining plastic grid trays in the trench, overlapping their adjoining edges to keep the brick spacing even. As you progress from grid to grid check that the field bricks are even with or slightly higher than the border bricks. When you reach the end of the path place the end border bricks.

When you are finished setting the bricks, pour sand on the surface of the walk and use a push broom to work the sand into the cracks between the bricks. Keep adding sand until no more will go into joints. Then give the walk a light watering with your garden hose to compact the sand between the joints, and spread more sand on the path. Repeat the process. After the first hard rain you will have to add more sand.

COMPOST BIN

Nothing makes more sense than composting your garden waste, because that takes the materials in your garden full circle. Even if you only use it to recycle leaves and lawn clippings, the time you invest in making a bin will be paid back tenfold in nutrient-rich organic matter to add to your garden. Instead of filling plastic garbage bags with these natural materials and then dumping them in a landfill, you'll enrich your plants and your yard for years to come.

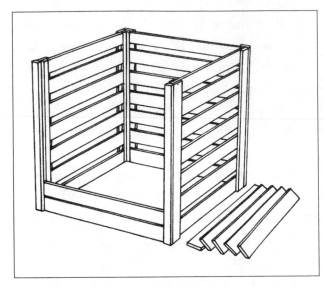

COMPOST BIN

grade lumber is quite all right, although the boards in direct contact with the ground will usually only last a year or so before they begin to join the compost. A couple of coats of a water-proofing sealer will extend the life of this grade of wood.

The materials list specifies enough wood to build one complete bin. You can add bins by building a back and side assembly and using one side of the original bin as a common wall. Some gardeners prefer two or more bins for composting different materials. For each side you add, include an additional three 8-foot 1 × 4s and one 8-foot 1 × 2.

This bin is a practical design using readily available materials, so it's easy to construct and assemble. Once it becomes a part of your backyard you'll wonder what you did before composting became a part of your gardening routine.

❧ Planning the Project

Since a compost bin is out in the weather all year, it should be constructed from rot-resistant wood like cedar or pressure-treated lumber. To keep this design as simple to build as possible only two sizes of lumber are used. To minimize lumber waste the materials list recommends what length to purchase for each part.

A compost bin is usually placed out of sight or in an inconspicuous area of the yard, so it doesn't have to be made of top-grade lumber. Utility

❧ Step by Step

The compost bin is composed of three identical sides. The basic dimensions are not critical but all the like named parts should be the same size. Cut the side slats and posts from 1 × 4 stock. Note that the side slats are cut from the 8-foot boards, the posts from 10-foot boards, and the front slats from a 12-foot board. The cleats are cut from 1 × 2 stock.

The cleats are glued and nailed to the posts with 3d galvanized or aluminum finishing nails. Place each cleat on the face of its post so that it is ³/₄ inch from one edge. This will place the cleat's other edge 1¹/₄ inches from the opposite edge of the post. Make six post-and-cleat assemblies like this.

Nail and glue the side slats to two post assem-

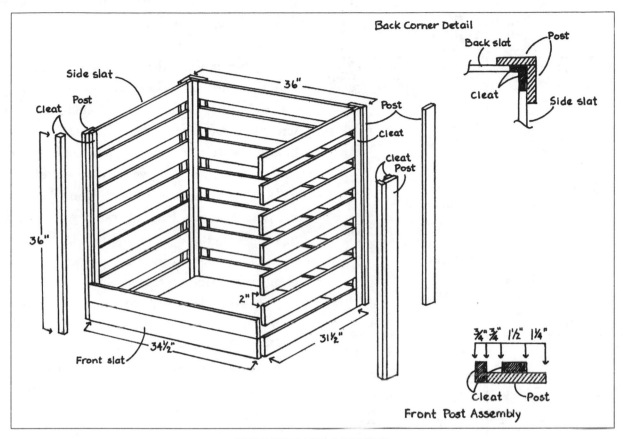

Back Corner Detail

Back slat

Post

Cleat

Side slat

Side slat

Post

Cleat

36"

Post

Cleat

Cleat

Post

36"

2"

Front slat

34½"

31½"

¾" ¾" 1½" 1¼"

Cleat   Post

Front Post Assembly

BIN PARTS AND ASSEMBLY

blies. Lay two post assemblies on a flat surface with the cleat side up and the 1¼-inch lips facing one another. Place a side slat between the cleats, align it flush with the top edge of the post, and mark its position on the post. Remove the board and apply glue to the post area covered by the slat. Replace the slat and nail it in place. Install a slat at the bottom of the post assemblies in the same way. Then use a carpenter's square to check that the frame is square. Or measure the distances between diagonally opposite corners. If the two diagonals are the same, the side assembly is square.

The plan calls for 2-inch spacing between the slats but absolute accuracy is not essential. Cut a couple of pieces of scrap wood 2 inches long and use them as temporary spacers in between slats when laying out their positions and nailing them. Work from the top down gluing and nailing the slats in place. Eyeball the placement of the last

Compost Bin
Parts List

PART	NUMBER	SIZE★	MATERIAL★★
Post	6	$3/4'' \times 3^1/2'' \times 36''$	PT wood
Side slats	21	$3/4'' \times 3^1/2'' \times 31^1/2''$	PT wood
Front slats	6	$3/4'' \times 3^1/2'' \times 34^1/2''$	PT wood
Cleat	8	$3/4'' \times 1^1/2'' \times 36''$	PT wood

Compost Bin
Materials List

QUANTITY	SIZE★	MATERIAL	PART
7	$1'' \times 4'' \times 8'$	PT wood	Side slats
2	$1'' \times 4'' \times 10'$	PT wood	Post
1	$1'' \times 4'' \times 12'$	PT wood	Front slats
2	$1'' \times 2'' \times 12'$	PT wood	Cleat
1 box	3d	Galvanized or aluminum nails	
or 1 box	$1^1/4''$	Galvanized all-purpose screws	

★ Sizes in the Parts List are actual dimensions; lumber sizes in the Materials List are nominal (stock) dimensions.
★★ PT: pressure-treated.

slat. It's close to the bottom and a small misalignment will not be noticeable. Assemble the other two sides in the same way.

The bin is formed by attaching three assemblies together, two as sides and one as a back. You can use either 3d nails or $1^1/4$-inch all-purpose screws. Screws have the advantage of greater holding power; in addition, they can be removed easily if you want to move the compost bin. Place nails or screws at least $3/8$ inch from the edge of the post. You can drive additional screws or nails in the back. Place them about 1 inch from the edge of the post on the back so they go into the cleat on the side post assembly.

The front slats are held in a slot formed by nailing a cleat to the edge of both front post assemblies. This cleat should be flush with the outside side of the post and extend to form a slot, as shown in a detail in the assembly illustration. The front slats slip into this groove. Put the first slat in place, then drive a few nails through the face of the cleat to lock the board in place and hold the two sides together at the bottom. The rest of the slats are left free so you can lift them out to easily work your compost pile.

STARTER SEED POTTING BOX

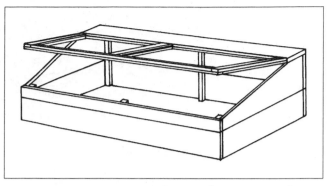

STARTER SEED POTTING BOX (COLD FRAME)

New seedlings need a safe and protected halfway house before entering the outdoors; here is a version of a cold frame to serve that need. Use the potting box as a place for new plants to harden off or to toughen before making the transition from a warm, well-lighted environment indoors into the garden. The sides offer warmth and protection and the removable plastic top lets in plenty of sunshine. The box is easy to build and can be raised higher off the ground to accommodate tall plants.

❧ Planning the Project

This project uses heavy stock, which can be difficult to transport. Unless you have a sturdy cartop carrier or a station wagon, have the lumber delivered. To keep construction simple this project uses butt joints with straight-cut ends, so cutting and assembly go quickly.

The potting box is exposed to the weather and the base of the unit is in contact with the soil, so pressure-treated wood is your best choice for building this project. When working with pressure-treated wood remember that the chemicals that preserve the wood are also toxic. Wear gloves and wash your hands after handling pressure-treated wood. Wear a dust mask to protect your-

self from inhaling sawdust while cutting this material and wash your work clothes separately from the regular laundry. Don't dispose of pressure treated lumber scraps by burning.

The parts of the lift-off top assembly are held together by the battens that run across the joints between the stiles and the rail so take care to cut the battens so that there are no knots close to their ends that may cause the wood to split. For best results drill pilot holes for the screws.

You can use either a rigid clear plastic such as Plexiglas™ in the lid, or flexible plastic sheeting, which is less expensive but not as durable.

❧ Step by Step

Begin by cutting the lower end pieces and the lower front and rear boards to length from 2×10 stock. Cut the upper end pieces from 4-foot lengths of 2×12 stock. A detail in the assembly illustration shows how to lay out the one angled cut in the upper ends. Cut out one end piece,

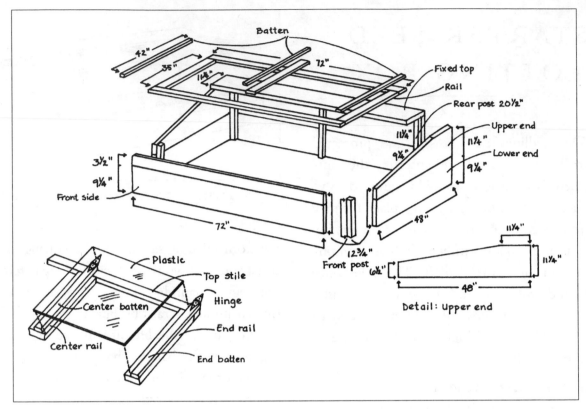

STARTER SEED BOX PARTS AND ASSEMBLY

then use it as a pattern to mark the second upper end.

Cut the upper rear board and the fixed top to length from 2 × 12 stock and the upper front board from 2 × 4 stock. Cut the front and rear posts from 2 × 2 stock.

Assembly of the basic box is straightforward. To construct the ends, place the upper and lower end pieces edge to edge. Nail a front post flush with the short, front end and a rear post flush with the tall, rear end. Use 10d galvanized nails.

Next nail the front boards together. Place the upper and lower front boards edge to edge, with their ends flush. Use 10d galvanized nails to fasten a front post to these boards in the center, 36 inches from either end. Drive two nails through the post into the upper front board and four nails the lower board. Join the upper and lower rear boards with a center post in the same way, but use four nails into each board.

The front and rear assemblies overlap the edges of the end assemblies. To prevent splitting, drill

$^1/_8$-inch pilot holes for 20d nails through the faces of the front and rear boards, into the edges of the end boards. Locate the holes about $^3/_4$ inch in from the ends of the face boards so they will go into the center of the end board edges.

Check that the corners are tight and that edges are flush before driving 20d nails into the pilot holes. After the frame is nailed together, drive some 10d nails through the front and rear boards into the corner posts to add additional strength to each joint. Complete the box construction by nailing the fixed top to the upper end pieces and to the top edge of the upper rear board part with 20d nails.

Cut the parts to make the lid assembly next. Make the rails and stiles from the 1 × 4 stock and the battens from the 1 × 2 stock. Drill $^1/_8$-inch pilot holes in the battens to prevent splitting when they are screwed to the rails and stiles.

Lay the three rails between the two stiles on a flat surface. Check that the two end rails are flush with the ends of the stiles and make 90-degree corners. Place a batten on top of one end rail, flush with its outer edge. Check that the alignment has not changed and then screw the ends of the batten to the stile with $1^1/_4$-inch galvanized all-purpose screws. Then drive additional screws spaced about 6 inches apart through the batten into the rail. Install the batten on the other end of the lid in the same way. Place the remaining rail in the center of the lid ($34^1/_4$ inches from either end), center a batten on the rail so there is a

Starter Seed Box Parts List

PART	NUMBER	SIZE*	MATERIAL**
Upper rear board	1	$1^1/_2"$ × $11^1/_4"$ × 72"	PT wood
Fixed top	1	$1^1/_2"$ × $11^1/_4"$ × 72"	PT wood
Upper end	2	$1^1/_2"$ × $11^1/_4"$ × 48"	PT wood
Lower front, rear board	2	$1^1/_2"$ × $9^1/_4"$ × 72"	PT wood
Lower end	2	$1^1/_2"$ × $9^1/_4"$ × 48"	PT wood
Upper front board	1	$1^1/_2"$ × $3^1/_2"$ × 72"	PT wood
Rear post	3	$1^1/_2"$ × $1^1/_2"$ × $20^1/_2"$	PT wood
Front post	3	$1^1/_2"$ × $1^1/_2"$ × $12^3/_4"$	PT wood
Stile	3	$^3/_4"$ × $3^1/_2"$ × 72"	PT wood
Rail	3	$^3/_4"$ × $3^1/_2"$ × 35"	PT wood
Batten	3	$^3/_4"$ × $1^1/_2"$ × 42"	PT wood

* Sizes in the Parts List are actual dimensions; lumber sizes in the Materials List are nominal (stock) dimensions.
** PT: pressure-treated.

Starter Seed Box
Materials List

QUANTITY	SIZE★	MATERIAL	PART
2	2″ × 12″ × 10′	PT wood	Upper rear/end; fixed top
2	2″ × 10″ × 10′	PT wood	Lower front/rear/end
1	2″ × 4″ × 8′	PT wood	Upper front board
2	1″ × 4″ × 12′	PT wood	Lid assembly
2	1″ × 2″ × 8′	PT wood	Batten
2 lb.	20d	Galvanized nails	
1 box	10d	Galvanized nails	
1 box	1″	Galvanized all-purpose screws	
1 box	1¼″	Galvanized all-purpose screws	
4	3″	L flat corner plate	
2	3″	T plate	
1	4′ × 6′	Heavy gauge plastic sheeting or	
2	33½″ × 42″ × ⅛″	Rigid plastic	
3	3″	T-hinge	

1-inch lip on either side, and screw it in place as you did with the end battens. Turn the lid assembly over and install an L-shaped metal reinforcing bracket at each corner joint and a T-shaped bracket at both center joints.

Turn the lid assembly over and staple plastic sheeting to the stiles and rails to cover the openings. If you are using rigid plastic, have two pieces cut to fit between the battens. Then attach them to the stiles and rails with 1-inch galvanized all-purpose screws. Drill pilot holes in the plastic to prevent cracking the material.

All that is left is to put the lid in position and install the hinges. Push the frame tight against the fixed top. Then place the outside hinges on the fixed top with the strap portion of the T-hinges aligned with the outside battens. Check that the hinge barrel is over the joint between the frame and fixed top and mark the hinge screw locations on the fixed top. Mark the location of the center hinge in the same way but align it with the center batten.

Remove the hinges and drill ⅛-inch pilot holes in the fixed top for the hinge screws. Then install the hinges with galvanized all-purpose screws which require a Phillips screwdriver or use rustproof brass or bronze screws.

After the hinges are screwed to the fixed top, mark the location and then drill pilot holes for the screws in the battens. Use the hinge as a template and drill these pilot holes 1 inch deep. Then install the screws.

To prevent overheating on sunny days you'll want to be able to prop the lid partway open. Cut several pieces of scrap wood in pairs of various lengths to use as props under the lid at the corners. Store these props inside the potting box when they're not in use.

BACKYARD ARBOR

An arbor is a freestanding wooden structure with a roof and open sides that creates an archway into a side- or backyard. A canopylike roof is attached to two sides that are installed permanently. When planted with climbing roses or a flowering vine such as clematis or wisteria, an arbor becomes the focal point of a yard, showcasing a cascade of colorful flowers. You can buy a readymade arbor or build the simple design illustrated here; either one can transform a featureless yard into a showplace.

An arbor is usually left in place all year round, so it should be constructed of rot-resistant wood. Both cedar and redwood are good choices for this project, as well as pressure-treated wood. If you decide to use pressure-treated wood remember that the chemicals that preserve the wood are toxic. Wear gloves and wash your hands after handling pressure-treated wood. Wear a dust mask to protect yourself from inhaling sawdust while cutting this material and wash your work clothes separately from the regular laundry. Don't dispose of pressure-treated lumber scraps by burning.

The arbor does not require a lot of wood but it will be a full load for the average car. Unless you

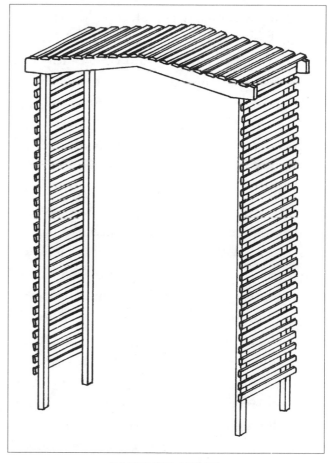

BACKYARD ARBOR

have a very sturdy roof rack or a station wagon consider having the wood delivered.

Outdoor wood projects require rustproof fasteners to prevent unsightly rust stains. Use either aluminum or galvanized nails on this project.

The lumber specified might not be available in the lumberyard where you shop so you may have to rip some boards to width or thickness or have the yard do it for you. Some yards may not stock $^3/_4$-inch-thick cedar or redwood, and pressure-treated wood is usually manufactured in $1^1/_2$-inch and thicker sizes. If you can't find 1×2 material to make the slats, have the yard rip $^3/_4$-inch-thick pieces from the edge of an 8-foot 2×6 board. Each board will yield six 8-foot-long strips that are $^3/_4$ inch thick by $1^1/_2$ inches wide. Have the lumberyard cut up at least four boards; you can cut the 8-foot strips to length for slats.

If the lumberyard does not carry 2×3 ($1^1/_2'' \times 2^1/_2''$) stock in the type of wood you choose, ask them to rip two $^3/_4$-inch strips off the edge of a stock 2×4. This removes $1^1/_2$ inches of wood from the edges of 2×4s for the leg and produces two strips that you can use to make slats. Of course you can also use 2×4s for the legs, which will not affect the construction.

The arbor is easy to build but it does have many small parts to cut. To make finishing easier, apply waterproofing or stain to the uncut boards. Then all you will have to do is dab some finish on the exposed ends after cutting the parts to size.

The arbor has 96-inch legs to allow you to set them into a 12-inch-deep hole. This is deep enough for most areas of the country, but if your area has severe winters you may have to dig deeper to prevent frost heave that will eventually throw the arbor out of square. In this case make the legs longer.

❧ Step by Step

Begin construction by cutting the 8-foot-long legs. They are cut from 10-foot 2×3 stock and the 2-foot cutoffs are used for mounting stakes. Cutting the slats to length is easy but tedious. Spend time making square clean cuts because the ends of the slats are visible.

The easiest tool to use to make the slats is a power miter box, which can be rented. The miter box produces very accurate square cuts and is safer to use than a regular circular saw. You can cut all the slats in an hour or less so the rental fee is minimal.

The arch pieces, which give the arbor its style, are cut from 5-foot pieces of 2×8 stock. Lay out each arch on a board as follows, then cut it to shape.

Decide which edge of the board will be the bottom and mark it. Measure 30 inches from either end and mark the center of the board along the top edge. Then measure at one end 3 inches up from the bottom corner and mark the spot. Draw a straight line connecting this point with the point at the center top to make the layout

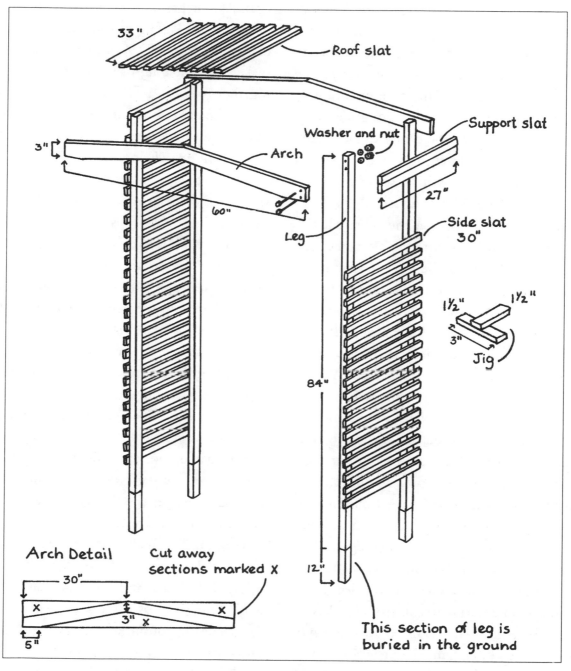

33"

Roof slat

Washer and nut

Support slat

3"

Arch

27"

60"

Leg

Side slat
30"

1½"   1½"

3"

Jig

84"

Arch Detail   Cut away
sections marked X

30"

X   X

3"   X

5"

12"

This section of leg is
buried in the ground

ARBOR ASSEMBLY

cutting line for the roof. Use a carpenter's chalkline if you have one, otherwise use a board as a straight edge. Draw another layout line from the other end of the board in the same way.

Lay out the lower part of the arch by measuring 5 inches in from one corner along the bottom edge of the board. At the center of the board mark a point 3 inches down from the top edge. Connect these two points with a straight line to form the cutting line for the lower edge of the arch. Make the same layout on the other end.

Use a hand or circular saw to cut along the top layout lines and then along the lower layout lines. If you use a circular saw you will have to finish the cuts at the center with a hand saw. Even though the cut is complete along the top layout lines the round blade of the circular saw will leave uncut wood at the center.

Assembly of the arbor is straightforward. Place the legs on a flat surface parallel to one another. Before you nail the slats in place, lay out and drill the holes in the top of the legs for the carriage bolts that will fasten the arch pieces in place. The first $1/4$-inch hole is located 1 inch from the top of the leg, the second is 1 inch below that. Drill the holes through the center of the edge of the leg stock. Drill a set of these holes in the top of each leg. The holes in the arch are drilled later.

Careful alignment and spacing of the slats is important for a good appearance. To help with this task, make an alignment jig using scrap wood. The roof and side slats overlap the supports $1\frac{1}{2}$ inches on each end and are spaced $1\frac{1}{2}$ inches apart. The jig can be made from a couple of cutoff pieces of $1\frac{1}{2}$-inch-wide slat stock. To make this simple jig nail two pieces of slat stock together to form a T. Check that the pieces are perpendicular to one another. Make two of these jigs so you can use them to align both ends of the slats during installation.

To use the jig, place the long arm of the T snug against the side of an installed slat and the short crossbar of the T is snug against the outside edge of the arbor leg. Put the slat you are installing against the jig and aligned with the outside edge of the T crossbar. This positions the new slat $1\frac{1}{2}$ inches from the installed slat and extending $1\frac{1}{2}$ inches past the leg.

Begin nailing the slats to the legs at the top. To help stiffen the side assembly and hold the legs in alignment, two support slats are installed at the top of the legs. The support slats are 27 inches long and are installed at the top of the legs without any gap or overlap. Nail these parts flush with the sides of the legs with 4d finishing nails. As you nail these parts to the legs be careful that the nails miss the bolt holes.

Temporarily install a slat at the bottom of the legs to hold them parallel while you nail the rest in place. Use the jig to maintain alignment and work your way down the legs. When you reach the slat at the bottom reinstall it to maintain uniform spacing.

The roof slats are installed on the arches in the

same way. Place the arches parallel to one another on a flat surface. Begin by nailing a slat on each side of the center and then place two temporary slats at the ends of the arches to maintain alignment. Install the slats from the center outward to the ends; respace the temporary slats when you get to them.

The roof assembly is attached to the legs with two 4¼-inch-long ¼-inch carriage bolts per leg. The easiest method of assembly is to put the side assemblies in place in the ground and then attach the arch assembly. You must dig two sets of post holes with their centers 26 inches apart front to back and 55 inches apart side to side; this matches the spacing of the legs. The holes do not have to be more than 8 to 10 inches in diameter and should be at least a foot deep. A post hole digger makes this job easy. Place 2 inches of gravel in the bottom of each hole.

You will need a helper to erect the arbor. Place the legs of one side of the arbor into one set of holes. Use a carpenter's level to check whether the side is plumb front to back. You will probably have to add some gravel to one of the holes to get the side plumb. Then use the level to make the side straight and plumb as you look at it from the front. Nail a 2 × 2 to one of the legs as a temporary support to hold it in position. Then do the same with the other side assembly of the arbor.

Place the arch on the legs and square up the arbor. Then drill the top bolt holes in the arch by using the existing holes in the legs as a guide.

Arbor Parts List

PART	NUMBER	SIZE*	MATERIAL
Arch	2	1½" × 7¼" × 60"	Cedar
Leg	6	1½" × 2½" × 96"	Cedar
Support slat	4	¾" × 1½" × 27"	Cedar
Side slat	50	¾" × 1½" × 30"	Cedar
Roof slat	18	¾" × 1½" × 33"	Cedar

Arbor Materials List

QUANTITY	SIZE*	MATERIAL	PART
6	2" × 3" × 10'	Cedar	Leg
1	2" × 8" × 10'	Cedar	Arch
25	1" × 2" × 8'	Cedar	Slats
2 lb	4d	Galvanized finish nails	
1 lb	6d	Galvanized finish nails	
4 each	½" × 4¼"	Galvanized carriage bolt/nut/ washer	
2 qt		Waterproof finish	
50 lb		Garden gravel	

* Sizes in the Parts List are actual dimensions; lumber sizes in the Materials List are nominal (stock) dimensions.

Insert the carriage bolts through the arch into the leg, place a washer on the bolt, and thread on the nut. Do the same in the other three corners. Double check that the arbor is square, then drill the hole for the second bolt at each corner and install the carriage bolts with washers and nuts. Finally, pack the leg holes with gravel, remove any temporary supports, and your arbor is ready for use.

POTTING TABLE

*W*hen you're working with plants, pots, and soil you need a large work surface to spread out your tools and materials. The worktable design shown here includes a waste area for debris, and storage space below for bulky materials, supplies, and equipment.

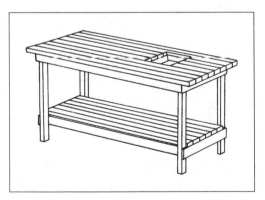

POTTING TABLE

❧ Planning the Project

If your table will sit outside most of the year, build it of redwood. If it will not be exposed to the weather you can use construction grade pine or fir lumber. The table is heavily constructed so it will hold heavy pots and bags of soil. It is best held together with all-purpose galvanized screws, which hold better than nails, but nails can be used. Use 8d galvanized common nails to construct the frame and 8d galvanized finish nails to install the top and shelf parts.

Most lumberyards stock 12-foot lengths of lumber. These longer boards tend to be of better quality. Hand-pick the lumber if possible, because you want the table to look nice. Avoid boards with knots along their edges that will loosen and eventually fall out. All the boards are used full width (no ripping is needed) so any edge imperfections will be visible.

The top and bottom stringers set the length of the table, so be careful to cut them exactly to the lengths indicated in the Parts List. Similarly, the seven braces determine the width of the table; they must all be the same length. Cut these parts precisely so the table frame will be square and sturdy.

❧ Step by Step

Construct the frame first. Cut the top and bot-

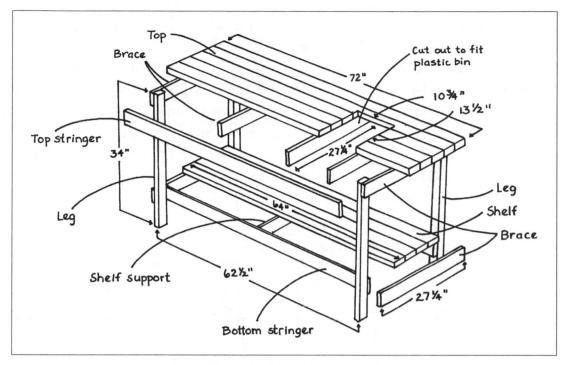

POTTING TABLE PARTS AND ASSEMBLY

tom stringers and braces from 1 × 4 stock. Note that the bottom stringers are 1½ inches shorter than the top stringers. The braces are all the same length. Cut the legs from 2 × 3 stock.

Begin by building the end assemblies of the frame. Lay two legs parallel to one another on a flat surface. Place a brace flush with the tops of the legs and set the legs to be flush with the ends of the brace. Place another brace with bottom edge 6 inches from the bottom of the legs. Check that the legs are flush with the ends of this brace. Use a carpenter's square to check that the legs

and braces are at right angles to one another. Then use 2-inch all-purpose screws to attach the braces to the legs. Use four screws per joint and keep them away from the ends of the braces to avoid splitting the wood. Assemble the other end of the frame in the same way.

The top and bottom stringers hold the two end assemblies together. Note that the top stringers go outside the end assemblies and the lower stringers go inside. Attach a top stringer to one leg assembly by screwing into the leg. Check that the stringer is square with the leg and that its end is flush with the outside of the brace. Attach the top stringer to the other end assembly in the same way. Use only one screw per joint for now so you can adjust alignment later.

Place the frame on its back, with the top stringer on the ground and attach the bottom stringer to the inside edges of the legs, in alignment with the lower brace. Then stand the frame up and attach the top and bottom stringers to the

other side of the leg assemblies, again with one screw per joint.

Set the frame so it is standing correctly on a flat surface. Check the alignment of the legs and that the corners are square. Then install three more 2-inch screws at each stringer–leg joint.

Now install the remaining three braces between the top stringers. Use two 2-inch screws per joint and space the braces equally between

Potting Table Parts List

PART	NUMBER	SIZE★	MATERIAL
Leg	4	$1^1/_2'' \times 2^1/_2'' \times 34''$	Redwood
Top	8	$1^1/_2'' \times 3^1/_2'' \times 72''$	Redwood
Shelf	6	$1^1/_2'' \times 3^1/_2'' \times 64''$	Redwood
Top stringer	2	$^3/_4'' \times 3^1/_2'' \times 64''$	Redwood
Bottom stringer	2	$^3/_4'' \times 3^1/_2'' \times 62^1/_2''$	Redwood
Brace	7	$^3/_4'' \times 3^1/_2'' \times 27^1/_4''$	Redwood
Shelf support	1	$^3/_4'' \times 3^1/_2'' \times 20^3/_4''$	Redwood

Potting Table Materials List

QUANTITY	SIZE★	MATERIAL	PART
7	$2'' \times 4'' \times 12'$	Redwood	Top/Shelf
4	$1'' \times 4'' \times 12'$	Redwood	Brace/Stringer
1	$2'' \times 3'' \times 12'$	Redwood	Leg
1	$5'' \times 12'' \times 13''$	Plastic dishpan	Bin
1 box	$2''$	All-purpose galvanized screws	
or 1 box	8d	Galvanized finishing nails	
1 box	8d	Galvanized common nails	

★ Sizes in the Parts List are actual dimensions; lumber sizes in the Materials List are nominal (stock) dimensions.

the ends. Check that they are flush with the upper edges of the top stringers, otherwise it will be difficult to install the top boards. Install the shelf support centers between the two bottom stringers.

The top boards overlap the frame 3 inches at each end and are screwed into the top brace at each end. To help position the screws draw layout lines $3^3/_8$ inches in from both ends of the top boards. Position first board so it overlaps the frame 3 inches at the ends and 1 inch in front. Attach it to the end braces with two 3-inch screws. Install the next board by butting it against the first board and screwing it into the end braces. Work your way back, installing the remaining top boards in the same way.

A plastic dishpan serves as a work bin. When cutting the opening for the bin, use the base of the dishpan as a pattern. Trace its shape onto the top boards. Make sure that the opening falls between two braces. There must be a brace on each side of the opening to support the ends of the top boards. Then drill a 1-inch hole in opposite corners of the layout lines and use a hand-held jig saw (saber saw) to cut along the layout lines. Remove the cutoff pieces and screw the board ends at the opening to the braces underneath.

Install the shelf boards with their ends flush with the lower end braces. Since the screw holes are close to the ends of the boards, drill $^1/_8$-inch pilot holes to avoid splitting.